MOTOR TREND®

CORVETTE FILES
Selected Road Tests & Features
1953–2003

From the editors of *Motor Trend*® Magazine

MOTORBOOKS
INTERNATIONAL

This edition first published in 2003 by Motorbooks International, an imprint of MBI Publishing Company, Galtier Plaza, Suite 200, 380 Jackson Street, St. Paul, MN 55101-3885 USA

Motorbooks International titles are also available at discounts in bulk quantity for industrial or sales-promotional use. For details write to Special Sales Manager at Motorbooks International Wholesalers & Distributors, Galtier Plaza, Suite 200, 380 Jackson Street, St. Paul, MN 55101-3885 USA.

ISBN 0-7603-1310-5

On the front cover: As part of its C4 offerings, Chevrolet developed the ZR-1 in 1988, which aimed to be the best-performing sports car in the world.

On the frontispiece: A *Motor Trend* tester opens up the hood to check out the engine of a supercharged 1957 Corvette.

On the title page: A Cortez Silver '69 427 Corvette paired with a '99 Corvette hardtop.

On the back cover: Zora Arkus-Duntov, the engineer who became the guiding force behind the legendary sports car, with a 1967 Corvette Stingray.

Edited by Leah Noel
Designed by Kou Lor and Brenda Canales

Special thanks to Larry Crane and Kevin Smith of *Motor Trend*® Magazine and Sean Holzman and Jack Westerkamp of PRIMEDIA Enterprises.

Printed in China

CONTENTS

INTRODUCTION

WALT WORON

Walt Woron

I T'S BEEN MY GREAT FORTUNE to nestle down behind the wheel of all five configurations of Corvettes—either before or shortly after their introductions. And, after driving countless models, I can truthfully vow—to paraphrase Will Rogers—that I never drove a 'Vette I didn't like.

This includes the whole gamut: from the bone-white, toothy-grinning, underpowered '53 to the sleek, viscerally-exciting C5 . . . and my all-time favorite, the '57 "Fuelie." In the context of their eras they were all—if not awe-inspiring—entertaining, unforgettable, and a blast to drive.

From its start in 1953, the Corvette has exuded an aura that sets it apart. Through its five generational changes, there's been no resemblance to U.S.-built or imported cars. Yet, it's not looks alone that gets the heart pumping and the juices flowing. After a stumbling beginning it was *performance* that became Corvette's first, middle, and last name.

In the early fifties, sports cars imported from England (MG, Jaguar, Triumph, and Austin-Healey) were fast attaining the stature of "in" cars among enthusiasts, those who were labeled "lunatic fringe" by Detroit. That was the climate when Corvette burst upon the scene: "the big American, flag-waving, apple-pie response" to those "durn furrin cars." On the street and on the track, it took but a few years to capture the hearts of that "lunatic fringe."

When *Motor Trend* compared the '56 Corvette against its main sales competitor—Thunderbird—we concluded that Ford was producing a "two-seater personal car," while Chevy was building something "a lot closer to being a sports car." That's the path Chevy followed for more than 50 years. And as such, it's the only modern make of car enduring as a nameplate for all that time. Its throaty rumble, scorching acceleration, and stirring looks meld it into a car that appeals across-the-board—to Traditionalists, Boomers, Gen-Xers, and Millennials.

Whether you call it a Corvette or simply a 'Vette, whether you prefer the simpler looks of the initial years or the "hot rod macho" look that followed, or one of the two totally-different Stingrays, or the modern, uncluttered sweep of today's C5—they're all Corvettes, one of the indisputable icons of modern automotive history, and they're all profiled inside these pages. Enjoy the ride.

Walt Woron was a founding editor of *Motor Trend*, working for the publication from 1949 to 1960. During that time he also held the concurrent positions of editorial director of *Auto Speed & Sport* and editor of *Sports Car Graphic*. After a public relations stint in New York with Peugeot, Renault, and Jaguar, he was asked to return as *Motor Trend*'s publisher in 1996, where he stayed for two years. As a freelancer in 2000-01, he reprised the original *Motor Trend* column, "Driving Around with Walt Woron."

DRIVING AROUND WITH WALT WORON

WALT WORON
Motor Trend, August 1954

We said in an earlier edition that the Corvette's performance was agile rather than startling and that the Buick Century could give it a hard time. Here's a neat conversion that combines the best features of each.

LATELY IT'S GETTING so that each time I pick up the phone I get a call that's intriguingly different. A month ago I had Jim Gaylord (of Gaylord-Shelton, Inc., Chicago, Illinois) on the other end of the wire. He quoted from an article in our June issue about the Chevrolet Corvette: "You say that performance of the Corvette is best described as agile rather than startling and that several American sedans, the Buick Century in particular, can give the Corvette a hard time. What would you think of a Corvette with a Buick Century engine?"

What I thought of it can best be described by the fact that I was on my way to Phoenix, Arizona (where Gaylord was at the time), by the following weekend. It's been a long, long while since I've driven as hot a near-production American car (by virtue of combination of two General Motors components: a Corvette chassis and Buick engine).

The engine had just been installed in the chassis and didn't have too many miles built up yet, so I didn't really force it through its paces. On the other hand, I didn't have to because it went like a bomb anyway. From a standing start, using DRIVE, I got to 60 miles per hour in 10 seconds (vs. 11.5 for the standard Corvette); using LOW, then shifting to DRIVE at a relatively low 4,000 rpm, I chopped this time to 8 seconds. To 80 miles per hour, shifting the same way, I made it in 14.5 seconds (20.2 for the stock Corvette). Top speed, when the car is thoroughly broken in, should be in the neighborhood of 120 miles per hour. I had it up to an easy 113.

Handling is not too unlike the stock Corvette. It seems to break just slightly sooner than with the Chevy engine, possibly because of one percent more of the total weight (3,100 pounds vs. 2,940 originally) being on the front end (1,720 pounds, or 55.5 percent). If anything, it stays a bit flatter in turns (probably because of Columbus double-acting shocks in front and a spacer used between the front spring coils to stiffen the spring). The one other chassis change that may have affected handling characteristics somewhat was the addition of radius rods running from the rear spring perch

Acceleration was not problem for the Corvette equipped with a Buick Century engine: from a standing start, using DRIVE, the car reached 60 miles per hour in 10 seconds (vs. 11.5 for the standard Corvette); using LOW and then shifting to DRIVE at a relatively low 4,000 rpm, the time was chopped to eight seconds.

Installing air deflectors, a multibladed fan, and moving the original expansion tank to left side of engine solved the overheating problems. The fan is from Chevy truck.

forward to the frame. It was felt that because of arching of the springs under full load, the spline might be pulled out of the driveshaft.

According to Jim Gaylord, "The engine just dropped into place." "Not so easy as all that" is the way Carl Grimes (Carl Grimes Machine Shop and Garage, Phoenix) put it. This was concurred in by Jeff Shelton, experimental specialist for Gaylord, who assisted Carl in the building up of the engine and its installation.

To install the Buick engine and Dynaflow transmission, the front Chevy engine mounts were removed (new ones being made up of Chevy pads), and special rear mounts were made up. To get clearance for the exhaust manifolds, it was necessary to roll the frame under. To adapt the open driveshaft, the Buick driveshaft spline was welded to the open shaft with a rubber seal on the torque tube ball joint clamped down to make a permanent seal. The transmission neutral switch mounts on the frame by using a Cadillac detent control rod back to the switch, hooking it up through the Chevy relay switch starter solenoid (completing the key circuit starter). The original shifting position and lever is retained without change.

The battery was moved over to the extreme right behind the wheel well and is shielded against the heat of the exhaust manifold. To adapt the 12-volt starter, a Chevy motor was encased in a Buick housing with the necessary drive unit. The generator is standard Chevy.

The biggest problem encountered was cooling, the sequence running something like this: Used Corvette radiator and Ford Six four-bladed fan—boiled in seven minutes; installed Harrison four-inch-thick industrial core (one inch lower, two wider), switched top expansion tank to other side—still boiled;

As part of one of many innovations in the conversion, the dual air cleaner setup carries a vacuum hose to reduce turbulence. The reworked Buick Century engine puts out about 240 brake horsepower.

Handling in the "Buivolet" Corvette is not too unlike the stock Corvette. Radius rods are installed between the springs and frame, a protective measure designed to lessen strain on the drivetrain.

installed Chevy truck six-bladed fan, changed radiator pressure cap from four psi to seven—still boiled; final change was canting of radiator and building of deflectors to direct flow of air through all of radiator instead of just bottom half, cap changed to 13 psi—cooling problems solved.

Installation of the Buick Century engine (200 brake horsepower) came after much modification: compression ratio of 9.5 to 1; polished, ported heads; matched manifold; ported exhaust manifold; Iskenderian 3/4-grind cam; solid valve lifters; Stromberg carburetor; a modified air cleaner modification with the intake forward to prevent excess turbulence into the carb; a DSM hot coil; and all ignition wiring shielded. It's estimated these changes upped the horsepower to 240.

I've seen some pretty nice conversion installations, but the Buivolet Corvette will stand up with the best of them. And not only will it stand up with them, it'll *go* with them!

Jim Gaylord briefs *Motor Trend* editor Walt Woron as well as Carl Grimes and Jeff Shelton, right, who aided in the conversion project.

CORVETTE V-8

WALT WORON
Motor Trend, August 1955

ONCE IN AWHILE a car that everyone likes to have fun with appears on the automotive scene. Such a car is the one that Don MacDonald describes as ". . . a bucket-seat roadster that will hold its own with Europe's best." That one was the first of the Corvettes.

After I drove one of these cars, I concurred in Don's opinion. Shortly afterwards, I received an invitation from Jim Gaylord to try out his "Buivolet" Corvette—a Corvette with a 240-horsepower Buick engine. I came away convinced that more horses was what the Corvette needed. It wasn't too much later that I was invited by Hank Rhoades to try out one of his neat conversions that wedded the '54 Caddy engine of 230 horsepower with the Corvette. This Chevillac caused me to go on record with the statement that "You can look for a much hotter mill [next year]."

I didn't quite make my prediction, for the "standard" Corvette still has a 6 of 160 horsepower, but a "modified" version using a 195-horsepower V-8 is available, which certainly lives up to that prediction of a "much hotter mill." The V-8 engine is the same as in stock Chevys, except for the fact that it has a powerpack of four-barrel carb, manifold, dual exhausts, plus a full-race camshaft that ups the horses to 195 at 5,000 rpm.

The first opportunity I had to drive this new Corvette was when my friend Lee Smith (of Los Angeles) loaned me his personal car. He wasn't anxious to have it torn up, but had just had it tuned (it registered 1,824 miles), so we both knew it was in pretty good shape. It was fitted with one of the new fiberglass tops (by Plasticon of San Gabriel, Calif.).

The first difference I felt between the Corvette 6 and V-8 was in the idle. The V-8 sounds more potent, somewhat like a race engine with its tough idle and exhaust tone like that from a boat. The first time I took off from a light was when I noticed a distinct difference. I knew it was going to be more of an accelerator than the 6 and might even come close to the hot Buivolet and Chevillac.

How close it came is apparent in a comparison of figures: The Buivolet got to 60 miles per hour in 8.0 seconds, the Chevillac in 8.3 seconds, and the Corvette V-8 in just 9.0 seconds (which is 2.6 seconds faster than the 6). It took only 15.8 seconds to get to 80 miles per hour (which is 4.4 seconds faster than the 6, and only a little more than a second slower than the other two bombs). In just 17.2 seconds, it was at the end of a quarter-mile, doing 81.5 miles per hour.

Acceleration runs were made with and without the plastic top, which made no measurable difference. A run up a 32 percent grade in LOW resulted in a speed of 37 miles per hour at the crest.

Its biggest improvement over the 6 seems to be at the lower speed ranges, for although it nicks the 6 by a sizeable margin in dragging away from a light, it goes from 30–50 miles per hour in 3.3 and from 50–80 in 10.1, compared to 4.1 and 11.2 for the 6. It's actually through the mid-range of speed (and engine rpm) that its power is the best. On a torque curve it's putting out its maximum of 260 ft-lb between 2,400 and 3,200, while still putting out 240 down to 1,600 rpm and up to 4,000 rpm.

The front-to-rear weight ratio is better on the Corvette V-8 than on the Corvettes with heavier engines and even slightly better than on the 6. The V-8 totalled out at 2,910 pounds, with 53.8 percent of it on the front end. Whether or not this slight weight differential (between the 6 and V-8) would make any handling difference is hard to determine, but it at least *seemed* like the V-8 stuck in corners a bit longer before the rear end broke loose. And when it did, it also seemed to take less throttle to correct it.

After I returned the Corvette to Lee with my raves at how well it went, I suggested one change: revising the plastic top

Just a moment after this photo was taken, the Corvette roared off on an acceleration run and clocked 0–60 in nine seconds.

From now on, better take a look under the hood before dragging a Corvette. If you see this V-8, you've got your hands full.

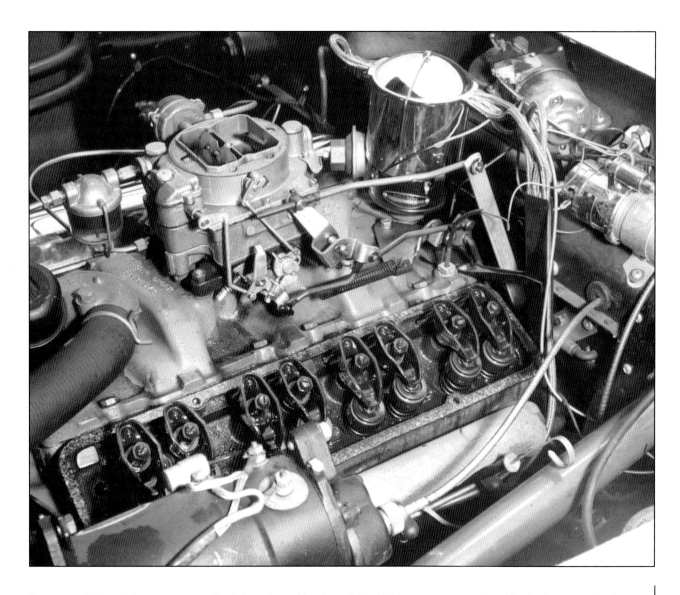

The accessibility of the components is obvious from this shot of the 195-horsepower engine with air cleaner and valve cover off.

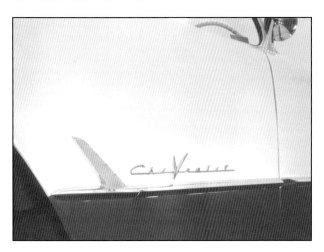

so that you don't bump your glasses against the top of the side curtain cutout each time you look quickly to the left. If I did it once, I did it 10 times. However, since plastic tops are still not factory-supplied (although factory-approved) extras, I look for Chevrolet to lick this problem (and a few others on weatherproofing) by an entirely new top design. The Corvette is much more than just a passing fad.

1956 THUNDERBIRD AND CORVETTE ROAD TEST

WALT WORON
Motor Trend, June 1956

THE ANNOUNCEMENT BY CHEVROLET that the '56 Corvette would have more power, wind-up windows, and better weatherproofing has, among other things, served to add still more fuel to an old duel. Where the Corvette may not have competed on across-the-board terms with the Thunderbird, the scales are now more evenly balanced. But don't get the idea that Ford has been lulled into a no-progress policy by its sales leadership with the Thunderbird; the No. 1 sales position is hard to come by and is jealously guarded.

To give the best possible comparison between these two Detroit-based "sports cars," we thought it best to drive the Thunderbird and Corvette side by side. We wanted the cars to be as alike as possible, but our plans didn't work out quite right: The T-Bird had more initial break-in mileage, which was partially compensated for by its also having power steering and the standard power brakes. It came with the standard plastic top and no soft top, so we (one person can't lift it off without marring the finish) took the top off and then kept both tops down during all testing.

With some prior acclimation to the two cars under our belts, three of us (Paul Sorber, our new staff member, Bob D'Olivo, our ace photographer, and I) climbed into the cars before dawn one day and rode off to our desert test site. Alternating between the two cars, we followed a route that led us through traffic, over a winding mountain road to the top of 5,710-foot Mt. Wilson, then dropped down onto the 2,000-foot flatlands of the Mojave Desert. Through the mountains we were pleased that the heaters worked as well as they did; with tops down we might have otherwise chilled ourselves into going back for the T-Bird's top.

BEHIND THE WHEELS THE FIRST TIME

Our first reactions to the two cars, of course, were those on getting in and out. They are pretty much alike in this respect, with the wraparound support cutting into your kneeroom

At the same position in the curve, and at identical speeds, the Corvette's better cornering shows up.

The Thunderbird's greater lean in corners could stand improvement.

as you snake in under the wheel. With the top up, it becomes more difficult, for you have to bend down, throw in a leg, duck to miss the top, scoot under the wheel, and again avoid the wraparound with your left knee. You should be under six-feet tall if you'll be driving either car much with the top up.

Once you get in the T-Bird, you'll find the seat is well-padded and comfortable, even for a long trip. On this particular T-Bird, the seat rose, lowered, and slid forward and backward by electrical power at the touch of a finger control on the door. Within a back-and-forth range of three inches, you can adjust the low-set wheel to your liking. Headroom, legroom, and shoulder room are good, but not exceptional.

The Corvette's seat is firmly padded and fits your back contour snugger than the T-Bird because of its semi-bucket shape. Each seat manually adjusts forward and backward, allowing you slightly less legroom than the T-Bird. You're also closer to your passenger, with less shoulder room, but you don't rub against each other. The nonadjustable racing-type, plastic-covered wheel sits close to you and is fairly high.

The T-Bird's instrument panel setup appears to have been thought out with more concern for driver seeability, what with the semi-circular speedometer high on the crash-padded panel, the tach close by and to the left, and the fuel and water temperature gauge below the speedometer.

The Corvette's speedometer, in its above-the-column position, is legible, but the position of the smaller tachometer in the center of the panel makes it almost useless. To see the fuel and water temperature gauges, you have to take your eyes well off the road. The advantage of having oil pressure and ammeter gauges instead of warning lights is somewhat lessened by their location on the far side of the centrally located tachometer.

The glove compartments are about a toss-up: the smallish T-Bird's compartment is a far right reach for the driver; the Corvette's upright box, in the center between the seats, is not useful except for the few things you can stack in it.

Chevrolet seems to have come closer to curing windshield distortion. Though some was noticed on the Corvette, the amount in the T-Bird was more annoying. Possibly because of our being closer to the windshield, there seemed to be even more distortion than on Ford sedans. Except for that complaint, and the bubble on the hood of the T-Bird, the cars have equal forward vision. Naturally, with tops down, all-around vision is excellent, marred only by the T-Bird's swivel-type rear view mirror, which can be pushed around to where it doesn't get in the way of forward vision. Glare caused by the blazing

Walt Woron talks with a member of the test crew before they conduct acceleration tests of the rival cars.

sun was noted only occasionally from the T-Bird's spokes. Driving into the sun, we praised Ford's foresight in providing narrow, padded visors and complained about the Corvette's lack of them.

TAKING THEM THRU TRAFFIC

Our next Thunderbird was more of an in-town car because of its power steering, but if you're of a mind to taint the Corvette's attempt at simon-pure sports car design, you can have it equipped with power steering, too. The stiffer steering of the Corvette is one of the features I like about it, though I dislike winding the wheel 3¾ turns to make a U-turn. Many undoubtedly prefer the driving ease (with a surprising amount of road feel) that the T-Bird's power steering gives it.

Whipping in and out of tight traffic situations, the cars do equally well. Unlike the feeling you get in many small foreign sports cars, you aren't domineered by the big Detroit bullies. The Corvette and Thunderbird are not as small as most sports cars, being little less in width

Trunk space is somewhat greater in the Thunderbird, but the continental wheel gets in the way. The compartment is much deeper than the Corvette's.

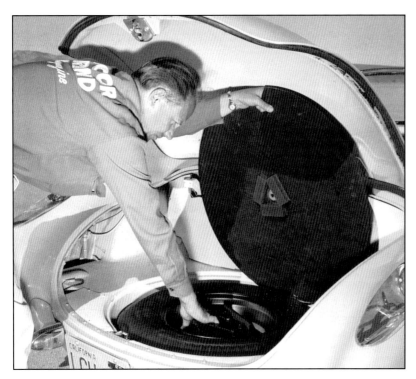

The Corvette trunk has flat floor with a spare tire that is awkward to remove without bumping your head. Despite easy access, there isn't much room.

and only a few feet shorter in overall length than their sedan counterparts.

Driving either car in traffic can't be termed an enjoyable experience, for you should have room in front of you to occasionally tromp down hard on the throttle. Not only is this dangerous in town, it'll cause a screech of rubber and possibly more than a raised eyebrow from the local gendarmes. It's more practical to wait until you get to open stretches where it's legally and safely possible to succumb to the urge of getting pushed back in your seat.

HOW THEY GO

It took quite a bit of experimenting by all of us to arrive at the best possible shift method for the utmost acceleration. More experimentation, as you would do with a Corvette or T-Bird if it were yours, might possibly trim some time off the figures we got. Those shown in the table indicate the most we could get out of these particular cars using this procedure: revving to 1,500 rpm in LOW, holding the car back with the foot brake, then suddenly releasing it and at the same moment stomping the throttle, shifting to DRIVE at 4,000 rpm in the T-Bird and at 5,500 rpm in the Corvette. By this method we shaved almost a full second off the 0 to 60 times with the T-Bird using just DRIVE, while we didn't improve the Corvette's time at all. In either car, DRIVE will obviously suffice for normal driving.

From scratch the T-Bird surges ahead, but two shifts (from LOW range to intermediate to high) against one (from LOW to DRIVE) for the Corvette allows the latter to catch and barely nose out the T-Bird at the quarter-mile mark. In the passing speed ranges, the Corvette was the Thunderbird's master, even when we tried a manual upshift from LOW to intermediate at 3,800–4,000 rpm instead of the normal 3,400 and

A dual quad setup dominates Corvette's somewhat roomier under-hood compartment.

higher rpms than the normal upshift at 3,800 from intermediate to high. Valves float in the Thunderbird at 4,400, not until much over 5,600 in the Corvette.

It's a surprising, but undeniably true, fact that neither our test '56 Corvette or Thunderbird had better acceleration across the board than its '55 counterpart. From a standing start neither of them gets off the mark as quick, apparently because of a loading up of the engine by over-carburetion, a characteristic common to most four-barrel–carbureted engines. When the engines clean out, they make up for some of the time they've lost; thus they get to the quarter-mile quicker, though they're not going so fast. In high-speed passing the '56 Corvette is faster than the earlier model, but not so the T-Bird. With both '56 cars it could have been a matter of lesser tune, or perhaps the '55s were hotter cars—cars that were made to run like clockwork by each factory's technicians.

The Thunderbird's engine, hampered with power equipment, is no direct comparison.

The floor-position shift on both Corvette and T-Bird seems quite natural after driving sports cars, which was probably the thinking in placing them there. Both quadrants are well marked; the T-Bird's is lighted at night, though without driving both cars intermittently as we did, there's not much to confuse you. In the Corvette, you can shift from L to D and from D to L with no strain and can't accidentally shift to R because you have to consciously press the lever to the left side and push all the way forward. The T-Bird has an added safety factor in that a knob on top of the lever must be pressed down to allow you to go from D (or N) to R. Unfortunately, this latch permits you to overshift into N when holding the lever in L and manually upshifting to D in trying to get better acceleration times. A modification could be made that would prevent you from going into N without pressing down the button.

An advantage the position of the T-Bird's lever has over the Corvette's is that you can rest your leg against it, at least until it gets too warm. In the Corvette, your throttle foot gets tired because you naturally rest it against the transmission hump, and since the throttle is straight up and down, you're pressing on it with only the ball of your foot. The T-Bird's lever jumped quite a bit on rough roads and vibrated some even on level roads, like the engine mounts were loose. Upshifts and downshifts were quite smooth in both cars.

During these acceleration runs, neither engine detonated and hot starts were easily made. Cold-morning starts were usually quick in the Corvette and took a little cranking in the T-Bird. Neither car heated up or even got up to 180 degrees.

Acceleration runs, and mountain driving, always bring out the shortcomings of the brakes, if any. Both systems were quite responsive and could be easily applied with left or right foot. There was some brake fade in the T-Bird, with quick recovery.

WHO'S TOPS IN ROADABILITY?

The general feel of the Thunderbird is unlike what you might expect from the car's size and appearance. Through turns it leans considerably, but after it reaches its maximum point of lean, it settles down and takes the corner quite well. When it breaks loose, which it does after an initial four-wheel drift, it takes considerable wheel correction and more power to pull out. Despite power steering, it retains a good feel of the road, enough to generally keep you out of trouble.

The Corvette, on the other hand, feels more like a sports car, with more steadiness and not as much apparent lean. The complaint leveled at it in cornering can't be laid to the suspension, which is good and firm, but rather at the carburetors, which starved the engine on a hard left turn; the right bank gets its share, but not the left one. This generally happens about midway in the turn, where you really need it. On right turns it was not quite as bad. The same was noted on the Corvettes at Sebring, except that they starved out in either direction.

When the Corvette's rear end does break loose, it's easier to correct than the T-Bird, though there are still too many turns from lock to lock for a "sports car." With just one less turn, making it 2¾ lock-to-lock, you could get through most turns without changing your grip on the wheel.

To really compare the cornering abilities of both cars, we took them through the same posted 20-mile-per-hour right angle (to the right) at 40–45 miles per hour. To compensate for any driver familiarity or error, Sorber and I switched between the two cars. For both of us the Corvette stuck in the groove exceedingly well, while the T-Bird drifted across the road, finally breaking loose and several times going off the asphalt.

The Corvette and T-Bird alike have a good sense of direction on perfectly flat, or even crowned, roads. When each leaves the asphalt, there is just a slight whipping. Hard frontal and side wind gusts had little effect on either car. Stiffer shocks on the T-Bird would be welcomed by drivers who push their cars more, though it would stiffen the ride. The wallowing at extremely high speeds (90 and above) makes it somewhat uncomfortable for driving; at lower speeds there's little to concern you. The difference between the two cars scems to be in the shocks, for the spring rates of both cars are quite similar.

On choppy asphalt you'll get some wheel vibration in both cars, but you won't hear nor feel any thud in the column. There's no tendency to swap ends on dirt washboard.

THUNDERBIRD vs. 'VETTE

PERFORMANCE

	'56 THUNDERBIRD	'56 CORVETTE
Acceleration:		
	From Standing Start	From Standing Start
	0-60 mph 11.5 seconds	0-60 mph 11.6 seconds
	quarter-mile 18.0 and 76.5 mph	quarter-mile 17.9 and 77.5 mph
	Passing Speeds	Passing Speeds
	30-50 mph 4.6 seconds	30-50 mph 3.6 seconds
	45-60 mph 4.4	45-60 mph 3.8
	50-80 mph 12.8	50-80 mph 11.0
Fuel Consumption:		
	Used Mobilgas Special	Used Mobilgas Special
	Stop-and-Go Driving	Stop-and-Go Driving
	12.7 mpg city and highway	12.8 mpg city and highway
	average for 650 miles	average for 650 miles

SPECIFICATIONS
THUNDERBIRD

Engine:	Piston speed @ max. bhp 2,637 ft. per min. Max. bmep 156.6 psi.
Weight:	Test car weight (with gas, oil, and water) 3,600 lbs. Front 1,780 lbs. Rear 1,820 lbs. Percent distribution 49.4 front, 50.6 rear. Test car weight/bhp ratio 16.00:1.
Prices:	(Including suggested retail price at main factory, federal tax, and delivery and handling charges, but not freight) $3,147.60.
Accessories:	Fordomatic $215, Overdrive $146, power brakes $34, power steering $64, power windows $70, power seat $65, radio $107, heater $84, convertible top alone $75, with fiberglass hardtop $290, safety packages $22, $32.

CORVETTE

Engine:	Piston speed @ max. bhp 2,600 ft. per min. Max. bmep 153.6 psi.
Weight:	Test car weight (with gas, oil, water) 3,020 lbs. Front 1,610 lbs. Rear 1,410 lbs. Percent distribution 53.5 front, 46.7 rear. Test car weight/bhp ratio 13.42:1.
Prices:	(Including suggested retail price at main factory, federal tax, and delivery and handling charges, but not freight.) $3,145.
Accessories:	Prices not yet released for publication.

HOW THEY COMPARE IN RIDE

The ride of the T-Bird is definitely softer. The Corvette's ride is more prone to transmit road noises to the driver and passenger. The T-Bird has a tendency to "float" over dips and bumps, which is comfortable at low speeds and not as likable at higher speeds.

Both cars bottom on intersection drainage dips if they're driven over at 30 miles per hour or above. After a dip of this type, the Corvette recovers its composure quicker. Each had a considerable number of body rattles, while the Corvette also had a vigorous cowl shake on rough roads.

The individual bucket seat of the Corvette is more comfortable for one passenger, but the T-Bird has the advantage of carrying an emergency second passenger in the middle, if he (or she) doesn't mind the transmission hump. The armrest of the Corvette is positioned somewhat better for the passenger, though with either car it's pleasanter to rest your arm on the doorsill; of course, this isn't the safest practice.

WHAT ABOUT FUEL ECONOMY?

In drives over the identical 650 miles, at identical speeds and in identical fashion, the Corvette and T-Bird got virtually identical overall gas mileage. Though 12.8 and 12.7 may seem unusually low, it's important to remember that we drove the cars hard and fast. Under less strenuous conditions you might expect up to 14–15 miles per gallon, though if you're like most people who drive such cars, it will be of little concern—except possibly for the next time you bench-race. Few competitors are so alike.

AND THEIR CONSTRUCTION?

The fit of the panels on the T-Bird was quite good, except for an occasional ripple in the body. The bumpers are sturdy, more like those of a sedan than those of the Corvette. The workmanship of the Corvette seemed to be on a par with that of the T-Bird. Common to fiberglass, there were a few cracks in the Corvette's body paint at a few stress points.

SOME FINAL CONCLUSIONS

The Thunderbird is pretty much what Ford claims it is—a "personal car," suitable for the bachelor, for the young or "young in heart" couple, or for the husband or wife as a second car. Its sales indicate that the people who are buying it are not necessarily concerned with its sports car attributes, nor are they overly impressed with unbeatable performance. A fact that's sometimes easy to overlook is that pretty big strides have been recently taken by Detroit manufacturers; since the introduction of the T-Bird in the fall of '54, several sedans have surpassed it in acceleration and will stay with it in the handling department. As a "personal car" it meets its requirements. For those who want to make it into a sports car, we would suggest firming it up, adding a good close-ratio gearbox, putting on bigger brakes, and lightening it considerably.

The Corvette is less of a personal car and closer to being, or easily becoming, a sports car. The sales philosophy of Chevrolet seems to have been more to compete with the foreign sports car market—at least until the Thunderbird came along. Now it appears that they're trying to split down the middle by providing more highway comfort for the average guy and/or the ability to make the car into a sports car by the addition of the modification kit (finned brakes, limited-slip differential, disc brakes, and heavy-duty springs).

Which one for you? Within $2.60, you can have your choice. Each performs a slightly different function, and each does right well for itself.

DRIVING AROUND WITH WALT WORON

WALT WORON
Motor Trend, December 1956

On the General Motors proving ground in the Turboglide '57 Chevy and fuel injection Corvette

WHEN PETE MOLSON and I drove out to the General Motors proving ground outside of Milford, Michigan, we wondered what treat would be in store for us. I remembered over two and a half years ago when Mauri Rose and I traded off taking the newly introduced Corvette around the "ride and handling road" and later steamed around the banked 3.8-mile oval. And I recalled later that year when the '55 Chevy was introduced there and we walked into the auditorium, the then–Chief Engineer Ed Cole remarked, "We've got something here I think you'll like." And later in the day he impressed me with his superb handling of the car in a power-on broadslide that saw us ending up in the direction we had come from. Then the following year, my treat was driving the Pikes Peak Hill Climb car, the Monte Carlo.

This crisp fall day I knew I'd get a chance to drive a Turboglide-powered Chevy and a fuel injection Corvette, but on what parts of the proving ground and for how long, I didn't know. Meeting us there were several engineers and proving ground personnel. The passenger car was an engineering prototype—that is, it had all the engineering modifications on the chassis and it used the '57 engine but still had the '56 body.

From the garage we drove out onto the oval track to warm up the car. During this time I recalled some of the changes between the '56 and '57 interiors: The newer circular speedometer is no easier to read, though the white letters on dark background are quite legible; all the instruments are shielded from shining on the windshield; control knobs are recessed for safety; the steering wheel is now semi-dish; switches would take getting used to for they're not marked or illuminated; heater controls are easier to read; and the publicized extra front seat headroom is there but not noticeable and ditto for the front seat legroom.

Once I put the quadrant in drive, I noticed absolutely no upshifting sensation. The only feeling you get that's at all like a shift is that if you suddenly lift your foot from the throttle while you're still accelerating, the blade angle of the variable stator

The 1957 Corvette is in the 135–145 mile-per-hour class.

quickly changes. You then get what feels like an imperceptibly smooth shift. Transmission and driveline noise at 60–70 miles per hour in this prototype seemed slightly higher than in '56.

Going down a 17 percent grade, I dropped it into HR (hill retarder), which immediately slowed it down from 40 to 20 miles per hour. I tried this several times more approaching sharp bends in the road; the slowing action was exceedingly quick—just like shifting down a manual gearbox. Highest recommended speed for downshifting is 40 miles per hour, though the engineers told me that they do it consistently at 55. They also told me that fuel economy with Turboglide is virtually the same as with Powerglide. I have no reason to doubt them, but we'll have the comparison figures in our upcoming road test of the new Chevy.

Ride and handling qualities of the '57 car seem about equal to the '56. If there is any change, it's difficult to detect by any seat-of-the-pants method.

After calibrating the speedometer as closely as we could, Pete and I ran some stopwatch performance checks (which also will be later corroborated by our road test). The engine in this Chevy was the 220-horsepower version, with four-barrel carb, dual exhausts, and 9.5:1 compression ratio heads. Here's what it did: 0 to 60 miles per hour in 10.1 seconds, 30 to 50 miles per hour in 3.5 seconds, 50 to 80 miles per hour in 10 seconds, and well over 100 miles per hour top speed. Compared to our '56 test car, the '57 is appreciably faster on all counts.

AND THEN CAME THE CORVETTE!

Dessert was saved until last (though little did I know that there was going to be a second helping). We jumped from the passenger car into the Corvette, the fuel injection development engineer accompanying me on these trips up and down the two-mile straightaway (with loops at both ends). Changes in the '57 Corvette being limited to the engine (at least for the present), I was mainly interested in performance. And perform it does!

From a standstill to 60 miles per hour, using first and second gears of the manual three-speed box, took a mere 7.2 seconds! To 80 miles per hour, still in second gear, took only 11.4 seconds. Not having a quarter-mile marker, we had to estimate and time between the .2-mile and .3-mile marks; our estimate is around 16 seconds. The end of the half-mile came up in 24.9 seconds. In none of these standing-start runs was I actually extending the Corvette. The 250-horsepower engine (9.5:1 heads, fuel injection, dual exhausts) was fairly new, so I kept it to a maximum rev limit of 4,500. Takeoffs were slower than need be too, because of the rear spring wrap-up. Popping the clutch would only succeed in causing the back end to jump, losing valuable time. I tried easing off the clutch pedal, which helped. The rear solution will have to be traction rods, stiffer rear springs, stiffer shocks, or a combination of these changes to absorb all that tremendous torque.

Smooth and powerful are the words to describe Chevrolet's new fuel injection system, standard on Corvettes, optional on all others with the large V-8.

Passing speeds were impressive at the upper speeds of 50 to 80 miles per hour, being 5.1, but 30 to 50 was little better (3.3 seconds) than the passenger car. Second gear was used in each case.

The function of the fuel injection system was notable. Starts were quick. Pumping the throttle doesn't pump raw gas to the cylinders, so you can't flood it. Throttle response is instantaneous. No maneuver could flood or starve the engine (and I tried with violent cornering and hard braking). Smoothness is a high point. I took it down to 200 rpm in high gear, then floored the throttle. Outside of a horrible pinging (it didn't yet have the vacuum advance that later models will have), the takeoff was as smooth as if it were in low gear, or in high gear at a much higher speed. Nothing but another short-stroke engine with fuel injection or a long-stroke engine (of which there ain't any) could give such low-speed performance.

The second helping of the dessert I spoke of earlier, came in the form of another fuel injection–equipped Corvette. This one had the 283-horsepower engine, with 10.5:1 heads, dual exhausts, and the special Duntov cam with solid lifters. This one had just been put together the night previous, but since the development engineer hadn't had a chance to unwind it, he said, "Let's go!"

I didn't need a second invitation, and since our time on the long straightaway was limited to just another few minutes, we had to make it fast. Fast we did. Down the strip one way with this 3.7-geared Corvette gave us 132 miles per hour, or around 5,500 rpm on the small and hard-to-read tachometer. Back the other way we tore at 134 miles per hour, and I'm convinced that it wasn't extended. With a few suspension modifications and more rugged brakes, the '57 Corvette bodes ill will for the foreign jobs in its road racing class. Who knows? It may start beating the Mercedes 300-SL, instead of usually running second to it. When its road racing record is coupled with this new-found performance, it's easy to scotch the rumor that Chevy is about to back out of racing. You'll see factory teams at Nassau, Sebring, and maybe Le Mans.

SAM HANKS TESTS FOUR CORVETTES

Motor Trend, March 1958

Here's a candid report on what an Indianapolis race driver looks for when he tries out a sports car.

When Sam Hanks announced his retirement from racing, having completed his most successful season yet, Motor Trend *asked him, "What next, Sam?"*

"Don't know," Hanks replied. "Just sort of sitting tight to see what breaks. I'll be doing something in the car field, though, you can betcha."

"How about running some road tests for us? You could start with the Corvette. We'd like to get an opinion of the handling and overall impressions of this car from a real racing expert."

"Don't know why not," came the quick reply. So here's the report in Sam's own words.

I HAVEN'T HAD lots of experience with sports cars, but from what they tell me, the Corvette's doing a pretty good job of passing for one. That's what made me so interested when I was asked by *Motor Trend* to give my opinions of the Corvette—*four* of them, no less!

I won't try to describe all the details of the cars to you, for you're probably pretty familiar with them. I'll just tell you what I think of them, from the place that I know best, behind the wheel.

It might be good to first tell you what the four different versions were. One was a 230-horsepower job with a single four-barrel carb and three-speed box. The second had 245 horses, two four-barrels, a three-speed box, and a limited-slip differential. The third was fuel-injected, with five more horsepower, but had a four-speed box. The last one was an all-out racing job, with special springs and shocks and heavy-duty brakes. It put out 290 horsepower from a fuel-injected engine and used a four-speed box and limited-slip rear axle.

To get back behind the wheel—the first thing I noticed about all of them was that they had seatbelts for driver and passenger. I don't know whether these were standard or not (*Editor's note: they're not*), but they should be. Anybody who's driving a car as hot as the Corvette ought to be glad to slip on a belt. I used them all the time, whether it was just driving around town or going full-bore around the course at Riverside Raceway. If I hadn't had my belt strapped on the several times that I took bad dips at high speeds, I would have stuck my head through the roof.

Being real critical, the first thing I objected to was the wheel position. To me it's too straight and too close to the driver. You don't get any leverage this way for fast cornering. It's like throwing close-in uppercuts instead of long-range jabs where you can get the weight of your body behind them. This may be the way they do it in sports cars, but I'd personally like the wheel further away and lying flatter like in the midgets and race cars I've driven. They could cut down the size a bit, too, so your hand would clear the door release knob when you're steering. Seems to me that this, and the armrest, would obstruct left arm movement and create a hazard at high speeds on a road course. Then again, it may be the sort of thing you get used to. Other people who drove the car didn't seem to complain about it.

The instruments are nicely grouped, and because they have white needles and numbers against a black face, they're easy to read—but only at night with light behind them. In the daytime, the convex glass that covers each instrument has a mirror effect, so instead of reading them quickly you see five reflections of yourself. I think if they made the glass flat it would be better. And while we're on instruments, I'd also like to see a bigger tach, even though this new location for the tach is a big improvement over where it was.

Two more things I think could stand improvement—then I'll get on to what I like about the car. The first one is the small sun ball you see reflected at eye level in the windshield. This is the result of the shiny paint on the cowl over the speedometer. If it was painted a dull

Sam Hanks (pictured here and below) gets behind the wheel of not one, but four Corvettes!

During his testing, Hanks gave the Corvettes a thorough workout and was frank in his opinions.

color, or padded, or flocked, they could eliminate that annoying reflection.

The second thing is a bit more serious, and that's the assist bar or hand grip across the curved-in area in front of the passenger. It's a good thing to hang on to, but it's not a good thing to bash your face or neck on. Even though it may feel soft on the outside because it's padded with some sponge rubber and is covered with leatherette, the main piece is channel iron that's 1/16-inch thick. It's tied in on each end to a heavy bar-plate that's bolted in place. This is the first thing your ole dad would take off any Corvette he'd own. If I replaced it, it would be with a solid rubber bar, firm enough to hold you, but soft enough to give.

I like the position of the clutch, brake, and throttle. They didn't take any getting used to and I never fumbled around with my feet trying to find the right pedal. This means a lot if you're doing any fast driving, particularly in a road race.

The gear shift levers on both the three-speed and four-speed transmissions are in a good position. The short stick is sitting right where you naturally drop your hand when you let go of the wheel to shift. I was particularly impressed with the four-speed unit because of its smooth operation and positive gear selector control. You can shift up or down just about anytime you want, providing you don't let the engine over-rev. You can even downshift to low at speeds close to 50 miles per hour!

The range between gears of the three-speed box seemed to be a bit greater, which allowed me to take the 245 Corvette around the Riverside course almost as fast as the two fuel-injected jobs. This was when the 245 wasn't

Hanks (on left) confers with Walt Woron during the tests at Riverside International Motor Raceway.

Positraction, or limited-slip differential, shows its advantages here. Although the right wheel is spinning in loose dirt, full traction is maintained as shown by the strip of rubber laid by the left tire. The car shown below has a conventional differential and demonstrates almost a complete loss of traction due to wheelspin in dirt.

A padded assist bar that is fine for passengers to hold onto around turns can become a hazard in a sudden stop. In this photo, the bar is removed, revealing a steel channel covered by a small amount of foam rubber and plastic.

A competition-equipped 290 (left), unlike other models, has rear brake cooling air duct openings in front.

running up to snuff, too. I didn't get a chance to take it around after it was broken in better and retuned, but if I had, I'm sure I could have equalled the time of the 250 easily. On another course it might be a different story.

One thing I'd do with any car as hot as the Corvette, and especially if I drove it hard, would be to adjust the clutch so the pedal would have about an inch of free travel after the clutch is fully engaged. This is a must if the car is to be used in competition on a drag strip or road course. This proved true when I took the competition Corvette around Riverside. After running three laps and booming down the long straightaway at 6,000 revs for the top speed check, the cockpit filled with smoke. It had that odd smell you get from a burning clutch, so I was pretty sure that was what caused it. It may also have been engine blowby, but in our acceleration runs later we also got the same smell after a number of clutch-offs. A proper clutch adjustment might have corrected this.

On the way to Riverside during one day of the test I was following one of the other Corvettes. I noticed that its rear track was as wide as the front and this came as somewhat of a shock. How could such a car handle any good, I wondered. It should be narrower in the rear if they really want a handling-bear, I thought. Yet I was surprised to see it go into corners and not get into any trouble. On the course later I found that it would break loose quite easily, yet the power slide was easy to correct. I soon found myself taking it around like I took my racing "stock" '57 Merc. Down the chute, brake hard, downshift, through the corner fast without going sideways, on the throttle coming out, snapshift to the next gear and wait—not too long—for the next corner.

Riverside is a tough test of transmissions and brakes. Outside of the trouble mentioned with the improperly adjusted clutch, there was no transmission trouble. Some brake fade and hard pedal were noticed after two laps around at an average speed of 73.5 miles per hour in the 250 Corvette. To show you what bigger brakes, finned drums, and air scoops front and rear will do for braking, I took the racing Corvette around for three laps at an average speed of 75.2 miles per hour and didn't get a bit of brake fade at any time. This says a lot too for the stiffer springs and shocks and the limited-slip rear end. When your inside rear wheel lifts slightly enough to lose traction, you have the other one biting in. This should make a noticeable difference in lap times. It's handy in mud or on slick streets, too.

There's one thing about the racing version of the Corvette: It's strictly not a street job. It's noisier, not only when you first start it, but all the time. It rides rougher, but is the kind I'd want to do any racing in. The brakes squeaked loudly in town, but that's because of the hard lining. If you're not interested in racing, you have a wide choice from among the other Corvettes—with or without fuel injection, four-speed, three-speed, or even Powerglide transmissions, hardtop with or without manual soft top, power-operated soft job, etc. I think my choice for an everyday job would

Rear brake ducts lead from the front opening and pass on the underside of the front fenders to ducts in the body.

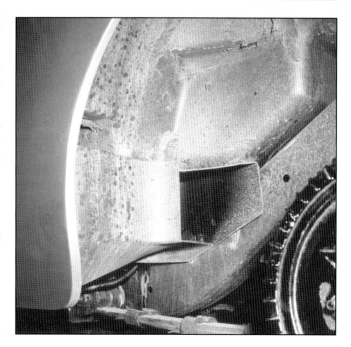

Discharge ends of cooling ducts in the body structure direct air toward finned, competition brake drums.

The rear brakes also have an air scoop for cooling. The lining pads are of a sintered metal and ceramic composition.

The steering pivot arm on noncompetition models, combined with gear and linkage, gives a 21:1 overall ratio.

The front brakes are also a heavy-duty type with finned drums and air scoops.

be either the 250 with fuel injection or 230 with single quad carb and three-speed box. I'd also choose the hardtop model because vision is better. When the soft top is up, there's a blank spot over on the right hind quarter.

You've got lots of power and good handling characteristics with all the Corvettes I drove. It's only natural that as you go up in horsepower, you go up in speed. The 290 had lots more zoom at the upper end than the 230 or 245, for example. It and the 250 also seemed to take the corners better, too. Or maybe—in the case of the 250 versus the 245—it was because of the quicker response you get from fuel injection and the greater flexibility you get in four gears over three. Any way you look at it, I think the Chevrolet designers ought to be proud of the style of the Corvette, and their engineers should be proud of a fine sports car. It's real great to have an American-built production car that's available to the public as a combination cross-country, city traffic, competition sports car. I'm impressed.

A fast steering adapter on the competition model lengthens the steering pivot arm, changing the overall ratio to 16.3:1.

Four-leaf rear springs and standard shocks give the noncompetition models a softer ride, but less stability.

The competition model has an extra leaf in the rear springs and heavy-duty shocks to improve handling characteristics.

230

245

THE FOUR CORVETTES

ACCELERATION

	230	245	250	290
0–60	9.2 sec.	7.6 sec.	7.6 sec.	6.9 sec.
Quarter-mile	17.4 &	15.9 &	15.6 &	15.6 &
	83.3 mph	91.6 mph	92.4 mph	95 mph
Half-mile	98.2 mph	109 mph	111.8 mph	114.9 mph
30–50	4.1 sec.	3.4 sec.	3.1 sec.	3.0 sec.
45–60	3.6	2.5	2.5	2.2
50–80	9.8	6.9	6.0	5.9

TOP SPEED

	103.1 mph	112.0 mph	113.6 mph	118.7 mph

Handling

(Time around 3.3-mile Riverside Raceway road course)

	3 min. 4.8 sec.	2 min. 45.0 sec.	2 min. 41.6 sec.	2 min. 37.9 sec.
	Avg. 64.3 mph	Avg. 72.0 mph	Avg. 73.5 mph	Avg. 75.2 mph

FUEL CONSUMPTION

Stop-and-Go Driving	11.6 mpg	13.5 mpg	13.6 mpg	13.8 mpg
Highway Driving	14.0	12.4	15.5	14.0
Overall Average	12.9	12.9	14.9	13.9

230 bhp @ 4,800 rpm, 9.5:1 C.R., single 4-throat carb, 3-speed manual trans., 4.11:1 limited-slip differential. (Car furnished by Enoch Chevrolet, 8730 Long Beach Boulevard, South Gate, California)

245 bhp @ 5,000 rpm, 9.5:1 C.R., two 4-throat carbs, 3-speed manual trans., 4.11:1 limited-slip differential. (Car furnished by Courtesy Chevrolet, 886 South Western Avenue, Los Angeles.)

250 bhp @ 5,000 rpm, 9.5:1 C.R., fuel injection, 4-speed manual trans., 4.11:1 conventional differential. (Car furnished by Harry Mann Chevrolet, 5735 Crenshaw Boulevard, Los Angeles.)

290 bhp @ 6,200 rpm, 10.5:1 C.R., fuel injection, special cam, 4-speed manual trans., 4.11:1 limited-slip differential, racing brakes, and suspension. (Car furnished by Courtesy Chevrolet.)

250

290

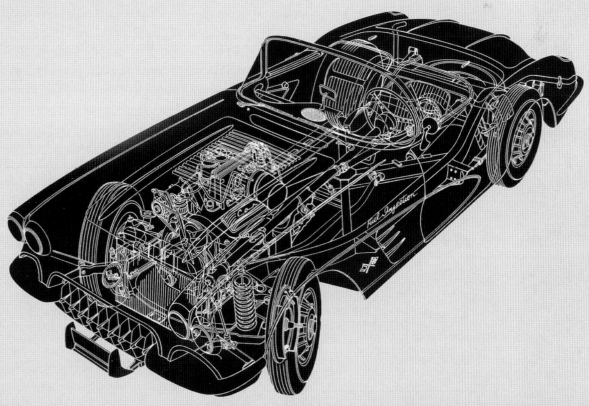

THE 415-HORSEPOWER BLOWN CORVETTE

CHARLES NERPEL
Motor Trend, June 1959

THE WELL-GROOMED '57 CORVETTE that owner Ernie Landel drove into the pit area of Riverside Raceway gave no indication that under its hood nestled a supercharged engine that had indicated 415 horsepower on the engine dyno. The rumble of the dual exhaust might have given away the fact that it was idling a bit fast for a street machine, but the absence of stacks or bumps usually associated with highly modified engines in stock cars is completely disarming. A closer look, however, revealed that those beautiful whitewall tires were special recaps, the rear ones carrying Inglewood "slicks."

As Ernie slid under the chassis to unbolt concealed Lakes plugs, the *Motor Trend* crew began hooking up test equipment to record acceleration times and passing speeds. This was not the first time on a strip for this machine as the owner and Les Ritchey of Performance Associates, who built the engine, had both made timed runs on southern California drag strips and reached some pretty definite conclusions. First, the slicks had replaced street tires because without them the wheels just spun. Second, the stock differential was locked up to get full power to both wheels, but there was still considerable wheelspin, even starting in second gear with the three-speed gearbox and a 4.11 rear-axle ratio.

Motor Trend's timing system requires an additional passenger other than the driver, to operate stop watches and record fifth wheel instrumentation, which is an advantage for traction but a penalty for weight. In addition, we removed the spare but replaced it with a 125-pound sack of cement located well back in the spare wheel well, hoping to overcome the extra passenger and cement sack weight with better traction and lowered elapsed times for the quarter-mile.

With Lakes plugs open, the quiet exhaust now became a full-throated roar from the blown 1/8x1/8 bored and stroked engine with a displacement of 328 cubic inches. A set of 270 heads, reworked to 8.8 compression ratio to take better advantage of the volume from the Latham blower that produced 8.75 pounds of boost at 5,000 rpm, and Chet Herbert 270 roller cam driving stock valves were the major modifications. Balancing, of course, and four Carter side-draft carburetors of the same type used on the old '54 six-cylinder Corvette, plus a lot of tuning and jet experimentation on the engine dyno, finally produced an engine that was docile enough for the street, but could give a good account of itself at the strip.

As the stock tachometer indicated only 6,000 rpm, we planned to shift when the needle passed this mark. It was going so fast, however, that our shifts were taking place somewhere in the neighborhood of 6,500. The additional passenger weight, plus our cement sack in the rear, aided traction, but we still left two streaks of rubber for 380 feet from the starting line as we recorded 106 miles per hour and 13.4 seconds for the quarter-mile. All of our times were within fractions of the electronically timed runs (driver only) made at southern California strips.

Motor Trend had a chance here to launch a rather interesting experiment. We have watched these young drivers do fantastic things with fast accelerating cars at the drag strips but were often concerned about the other phases of their fast driving of stockers on the highway.

The owner of this Corvette, Ernie Landel, is 20 years old and works in the container manufacturing plant managed by his father. Every dime Ernie makes goes into automobiles, and drag racing is just a way of preparing himself for his real ambition—road racing. True, he drives fast on occasion on the highway, but being a law-abiding motorist, he never really goes as hard as is necessary in competition. Here was Riverside Raceway, an internationally known road-racing circuit that had seen some of the best drivers in the business learn a new respect for this type of racing. And . . . here was this young eager driver with a hot car and the course all to himself. How would he handle braking and cornering problems?

Bouncing slicks left ladder tracks on the dragstrip surface before a sack of cement was placed in spare tire well to reduce wheelhop.

The Inglewood slicks are well camouflaged by white sidewall tires. The bicycle wheel is part of instrumentation for timing speed runs.

No bumps or stacks mark the '57 Corvette as a real powerhouse.

Owner Ernie Landel explains to Charles Nerpel how it was necessary to cut and remove only one hood reinforcing strip to clear the top-mounted supercharger.

A few laps under *Motor Trend*'s supervision to point out the tricky turns, the cut-off markers, and how to downshift to conserve brakes and aid cornering—and Ernie was turned loose on his own. Five erratic laps later he pulled into the pits, excited and amazed. "I had no idea that a car had to do anything but go . . ." So we waved him on for some more practice, despite some concern he expressed about the locked rear end and slick-type tires. These were actually aiding him to reduce lap times in the corners as the 4.11 rear end kept straightway speeds down to about 130 miles per hour. By the time he decided to quit, due to depletion of fuel (gas consumption about five miles per gallon), the tire dust that seeped up from behind the seats was well imbedded in the rivulets of perspiration running down from beneath his crash helmet.

Here was a real happy young man, but his conversation, normally dominated by such things as "wheelspin," "quarter-mile," etc., suddenly became full of "drift," "downshift," "braking," "cut-off points," "SS conversion kits for suspension," "steering," and "wheel position." In plain words, he now not only wants to go, but stop and turn, as well. We think we made our point.

A few things in review about such conversions: No one is ever satisfied with such modifications unless he can use them to the fullest. Locked rear ends and slicks have certain limitations for street use such as the need to make wide turns and be content with rapid tire wear. To be able to install this combination easily for drag racing has very definite advantages, and Ernie intends to revert to conventional rear end for street use. While this engine does behave well in traffic, it is very hard to start and for assurance that there will be enough current always available for this purpose, two batteries should be installed. To be certain of a plentiful fuel supply, an extra electric pump is used at the tank that pumps to the regular mechanical engine pump. Only top premium gasoline works well in this engine, and around town the car has a hard time getting better than 8.5 miles per gallon, but it sure does go-o-o-o . . . .

1957 CORVETTE

ACCELERATION (from standing start)

	0-45	0-60	Quarter-mile
	3.6 sec.	5.6	13.4 & 106 mph

PASSING SPEEDS

	30-50	45-60	50-80
	1.6 sec.	1.8 sec.	3.8 sec.

With Lakes plugs open, the quiet exhaust quickly became a full-throated roar.

CORVETTE
FULL-RANGE
ROAD TEST

Motor Trend, September 1961

THE ONLY MASS-PRODUCED sports car manufactured in the United States is the distinction still retained by the Corvette. In all of its many forms, it definitely possesses the characteristics and personality necessary to bear the sports car label. It matters not whether someone wants a two-seater merely for transportation or an all-out racing machine—there is a Corvette to fit his desires, no matter how extreme.

In order to sample at least a couple of Corvette variations, we tested two automobiles that were identical except for color and engine option. The more conservative of the two, ironically, was painted a bright red both inside and out—even the carpeting and upholstering matched the paint. Specifically, all that made it more conservative was the installation of the mild, 230-horsepower engine, which is the lowest-powered unit available.

The more sedate-appearing white test car displayed an identical interior except for one important instrument panel feature, a tachometer redlined at 6,500 rpm instead of 5,300. Even before the key is turned to start the engine, this sliver of red is a dead giveaway that a 315-horsepower fuel injection engine lies ahead of the four-speed gearbox.

This power and drivetrain package, though similar to previous years, received some important alterations in the 1961 version. Intake valves and ports were both enlarged to improve breathing and help raise the output from the previous maximum of 290 horsepower. The superb four-speed gearbox, fitted to both cars, now has a completely aluminum case instead of just using the light metal in the tail-shaft housing.

An underhood view reveals one other important area in which aluminum is now being used—the radiator and top tank. The tank is divorced from the radiator and is bracketed to the engine, allowing a more graceful hood slope. In this case the use of aluminum cut the radiator weight in half.

Seated in the cockpit, a 1961 underbody contour change becomes apparent—the transmission hump has been narrowed so that the driver's right leg and throttle foot don't appear to be as cramped.

The instrument panel is still one of the very few that contain a full complement of instruments. The only warning lights that appear are for the hand brake and high beam of the headlights. The brake light is a new addition for 1961; both lights spell out their purposes luminously so that even an unfamiliar driver will understand their purposes. The centrally located tachometer is in a very practical position, just ahead of the steering wheel hub. Forward and higher, the speedometer dominates the center of the panel proper. In certain types of competition events, it would be nice if the tach and speedo could trade places so that the rev counter could be bigger.

Driving both Corvettes definitely demonstrated that their character is very much the sports variety, even though they are very plush vehicles. Tufted carpeting and considerable use of chrome trim, including pattern chromed teardrop-shaped panels attached to the doors and kickpads, create an air of luxury. When you grasp the steering wheel and negotiate a turn at high speed, and when you shift the four-speed gearbox, you completely lose sight of your luxurious environment and realize that you are driving a true sports car.

Both test cars were not fitted with power steering, so they inspired a feeling of confidence when cornering. The fast steering ratio, which required a little better than three and a half turns of the steering wheel from lock-to-lock, might be too stiff for some women, but any driver that appreciates the security of having maximum feel of the car will be very happy with it. For those that don't wish to flex their muscles, power steering is available.

When a driver is seated in the cockpit, a 1961 Corvette's underbody contour change becomes apparent—the transmission hump has been narrowed so that the driver's right leg and throttle foot don't appear to be as cramped.

No matter what you pay for a sports car, whether it be in the four-figure or five-figure bracket, there is none that shifts more easily and more consistently than the Corvette four-speed box. Being synchromesh in all forward speeds, all gears can be selected in any sequence of up- or downshifting without gear clash. The best feature of all is the reverse gear lockout, which is controlled by lifting a couple of prongs on the side of the shift lever about two inches below the knob. It is impossible to shift into reverse unless these prongs are raised, so one need never fear hitting reverse when shifting into first. Without the lockout, many drivers have a tendency to move the lever too far to the right in their avoidance of reverse, with the net result that the lever gets hung up between first and third, so we can't offer enough praise for this device.

The Corvette's cornering ability is definitely in the superior category and for many reasons. The car has a fairly low center of gravity, moderately stiff suspension, and a stiff front

Acceleration tests of the two Corvettes showed most difference exists not at low and mid speeds, but at top end.

The familiar interior of the sports car has all necessary instruments arranged in a near-ideal manner. The gearbox is one of the best. Note the lockout latch for reverse.

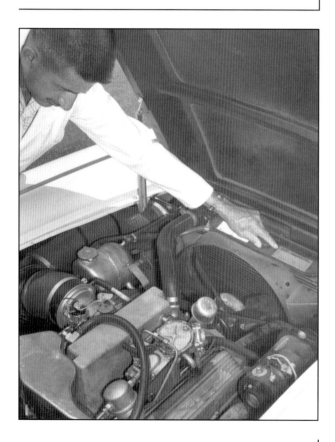

A look inside the engine compartment of the fuel-injected Corvette reveals a new use of aluminum. Both radiator and top tank are of the lighter metal.

stabilizer bar. Engineering wisely sacrificed softness of ride for safety in this machine. The body appears to lean a minimum amount during fast cornering, probably because of the heavy torsional stabilizer bar and lighter unit of the same type on the rear suspension. Though this rear bar doubtless contributes to flat cornering, it has a detrimental effect on rear wheel adhesion. In a hard corner, it has a tendency to take weight off the inside rear wheel, causing the outside rear wheel to be called upon to offer the majority of the resistance to side thrust. This is not good racing practice for power-on cornering. In actual driving, though the back end wasn't uncontrollable, it did start drifting earlier than the other characteristics of the car would indicate.

One of the pleasantest things about cornering a Corvette with the 315-horsepower engine is the behavior of the fuel injection system. Since it is not dependent on its float bowl level for fuel metering as in a four-barrel carburetor, it acts completely insensitive to motion. In maneuvers that would cause a four-barrel–equipped engine to lose power or die completely, the fuel-injected engine purrs like nothing was happening. Due to the fact that injector nozzles spray the fuel into the ports, much larger throttle openings can be tolerated at low rpm than with carburetion. One simple butterfly is all that is necessary to control the system instead of a complex of progressive linkage and many throttles. Port distribution also eliminates the necessity for a heat riser, thereby improving volumetric efficiency by allowing a cooler, more dense charge to enter the cylinder.

When comparing the performance of the two engine options tested, we should not lose sight of the fact that the difference goes far beyond the single area of carburetion. Though all Corvette engines have a displacement of 283 cubic inches, there is much that is done in the way of altering breathing ability to produce variations in output. The mildest engine is fitted with a hydraulic-lifter cam that limits rpm to the passenger-car range and provides only 250 degrees of valve-opening duration on both the intake and exhaust valves. An overlap duration of 28 degrees in conjunction with the use of a four-barrel carburetor makes the 230-horsepower engine behave like the best-mannered passenger car.

The 315-horsepower engine absolutely won't idle under 700 rpm and is most consistent in the 800-to-900-rpm range because of the combined effects of 66 degrees of valve overlap and the inability of the fuel injection system to maintain pressure within its lines at low rpm. The overall duration of this engine's cam provides both valves with 287 degrees of opening.

Due to the 72-degree late closing of intake valves in the hotter engine, plus more accurate fuel distribution from the injection system, an 11:1 compression ratio requires no special concessions whatsoever. The short timing and carburetion system of the mildest engine limits its compression to a 9.5:1 ratio.

MOTOR TREND TEST DATA

TEST CAR:	Corvette
BODY TYPE:	2-door convertible
BASE PRICE:	$4,109
ENGINE TYPE:	V-8
DISPLACEMENT:	283 ci
COMPRESSION RATIO:	9.5:1
CARBURETION:	Single 4-barrel
HORSEPOWER:	230 @ 4,800 rpm
TRANSMISSION:	4-speed manual
REAR-AXLE RATIO:	3.70:1
GAS MILEAGE:	11 to 15 mpg
ACCELERATION:	0-30 mph in 3.8 sec., 0-45 mph in 5.7 sec., and 0-60 mph in 8.3 sec.
SPEEDOMETER ERROR:	Indicated 30, 45, and 60 mph are actual; 30, 45, and 60 mph, respectively
ODOMETER ERROR:	Indicated 100 miles is actually 95 miles
WEIGHT-POWER RATIO:	13 lbs. per hp
HP PER CI:	.81

MOTOR TREND TEST DATA

TEST CAR:	Corvette
BODY TYPE:	2-door convertible
BASE PRICE:	$4,636
ENGINE TYPE:	V-8
DISPLACEMENT:	283 ci
COMPRESSION RATIO:	11.0:1
CARBURETION:	Fuel injection
HORSEPOWER:	315 @ 6,200 rpm
TRANSMISSION:	4-speed manual
REAR-AXLE RATIO:	3.70:1
GAS MILEAGE:	10 to 14 mpg
ACCELERATION:	0-30 mph in 3.5 sec., 0-45 mph in 5.4 sec., and 0-60 mph in 7.4 sec.
SPEEDOMETER ERROR:	Indicated 30, 45, and 60 mph are actual; 29, 43½ and 58 mph, respectively
ODOMETER ERROR:	Indicated 100 miles is actually 95 miles
WEIGHT-POWER RATIO:	9.6 lbs. per hp
HP PER CI:	1.1

A good comparison of the performance potential of the two cars cannot be gained by merely comparing their low-speed and midrange performance figures because there really isn't a large numerical difference. However, a time of 8.3 seconds 0 to 60 miles per hour for the mild engine as compared to 7.4 seconds for the hot version will impress those that have experience in the field of acceleration testing. A quarter-mile run would show a very large difference between the two.

In all ranges of acceleration, both cars would make more impressive showings if they had special tires and rear end gears more favorable than 3.7:1. This is actually the smallest ratio available in a Corvette, equipped as the test cars were, with a four-speed transmission and limited-slip differential combination.

The Corvette's cornering ability is definitely in the superior category and for many reasons. The car has a fairly low center of gravity, moderately stiff suspension, and a stiff front stabilizer bar.

Though our road test dealt only with the mildest and hottest engines available, there are three other optional power plant choices possible: a 245-horsepower, 270-horsepower, and a 275-horsepower. The most conservative of the three is the same as the 230-horsepower engine, except that it is fitted with dual–four-barrel carburetion. The 270-horsepower engine follows the same trend, but in addition to the carburetion a longer-duration mechanical-lifter cam replaces the hydraulic assembly of the two milder engines. At the other end of the list, the 275-horsepower option is the same as the hottest fuel injection job. It shares the same 11:1 compression but uses a mild hydraulic-lifter cam.

Three transmissions are available with the two mildest engines: a three-speed, four-speed, and Powerglide. The three hottest engines can be ordered only with three-speed or four-speed boxes because of their fast idle speeds.

Mechanical options aren't the only ones available, nor have we listed all of them—convenience items like power assists, convertible tops, and removable hardtops make it possible to order a Corvette to fit any individual preference.

A single four-barrel provides carburetion for the mildest of the Corvettes. With 230 horsepower, it is designed for best performance at normal passenger-car ranges.

No matter what you pay for a sports car, whether it be in the four-figure or five-figure bracket, there is none that shifts more easily and more consistently than the Corvette four-speed box.

CORVETTE STING RAY

JIM WRIGHT
Motor Trend, May 1963

For the first time in its 10-year history,
the Corvette STING RAY is . . .

I N SUCH DEMAND THAT the factory has had to put on a second shift and still can't begin to supply cars fast enough. The waiting period is at least 60 days, and dealers won't "deal" a bit on either coupes or roadsters. Both are going for the full sticker price, with absolutely no discount and very little (if any) over-allowance on trade-ins.

This is a healthy situation for Chevrolet, and we're happy to see the 'Vette get the public acceptance we've always felt it deserved. Yet after giving the new one a thorough shakedown, we can't help but let our thoughts stray back to last year's road test and one statement in particular we made.

It had to do with how the factory has never really made any big profits on the Corvette, but that Chevy brass was more than satisfied as long as it carried its performance image and prestige over to the bread-and-butter lines. We also ventured an opinion that as long as the factory kept building the car on this basis it would be a great automobile, but if they ever put it on a straight dollar-profit basis, the Corvette would probably be ruined.

Well, they haven't ruined it yet, but our test car (as well as several others we've checked out) showed definite signs that the factory might be getting more interested in dollars than in prestige. From the important styling and all-around performance angles, the new Sting Ray is an even greater car than its predecessors. But for a car that sells in the $4,500–6,000 range, it doesn't reflect the degree of quality control we feel it should.

To begin with, there still seems to be some difficulty in manufacturing a really smooth fiberglass body. While this isn't too apparent in a light-colored car, it becomes all too noticeable in some of the darker ones. When the light hits these from almost any angle, there's a definite rippled effect. The doors on our test car had gaps around them that were wider than they should have been. The doors didn't line up too well, either. This was also true of the hood.

In the past, we've always been impressed with interior trim in most GM products. The moldings usually look as if they've been very carefully designed for a precision fit. To

From the important styling and all-around performance angles, the new Sting Ray is an even greater car than its predecessors.

our eye, the Sting Ray coupe's interior had an unfinished look. Not that the upholstery and carpet materials weren't top grade—they were—but the various door and window moldings aren't too well designed in the first place, and it doesn't take much laxity of quality control on the assembly line to make them look really bad. While these aren't earthshaking faults or defects, and have absolutely nothing to do with the operation of the car, they are of the sort that a discerning owner and driver will be constantly aware of.

For the first time, the Corvette is available with power steering and power brakes. We didn't have either on the test car, but we've driven several set up this way. Combined with one of the smaller engines and Powerglide transmission, these power accessories make the Sting Ray docile enough for little old ladies or any other types interested in a nice, quiet, Sunday-go-to-meeting car.

The basic powertrains are carried over from last year and include four engines of 250, 300, 340, and 360 horsepower. Powerglides are available with either the 250- or 300-horsepower engines. Basic transmission with all engines is a three-speed manual, with four-speed available optionally. The 340- and 360-horsepower engines use the close-ratio (2.20:1 low gear) four-speed. Six rear-axle ratios are available and include the 3.36 (standard with three-speeds and Powerglide), 3.70 (standard with four-speed transmission), plus other gear sets of 3.08:1, 3.55:1, 4.11:1, and 4.56:1.

The Rochester fuel injection has been redesigned again this year. The 327-ci V-8 delivers 360 horsepower at 6,000 rpm and has good torque output.

Said to be the result of extensive wind-tunnel testing, the Sting Ray's boat tail may give less wind resistance, but it definitely hampers vision.

The *Motor Trend* test car was equipped with the fuel injection, 360-horsepower mill, four-speed, and 3.70:1 Positraction rear axle. Sintered-iron brake linings and heavy-duty suspension completed the option package.

On a straight acceleration basis, there's very little difference between last year's car and the new one. Our quarter-mile times are within fractions of what they were last year. The only real difference is that the new one doesn't have quite the wheelspin (with stock tires) that the old rigid-axle car had. The 0–30, 0–45, and 0–60-mile-per-hour steps averaged 2.9, 4.2, and 5.8 seconds, while our average time through the quarter-mile traps was 102 miles per hour, with a 14.5-second elapsed time. Top speed was an honest 130 miles per hour, with the tachometer reading 6,000 rpm. A course longer than the Riverside Raceway back-stretch would've produced something very close to the Sting Ray's theoretical top speed of 140–142 miles per hour (with 3.70 gears) because the engine was still winding when we had to back off. The 360-horsepower engine is set up like any well-designed racing engine, and it's very strong throughout the entire rpm range.

This is one of the few high-output engines that can deliver decent gas mileage without being babied. Out on the highway, we averaged slightly better than 18 miles per gallon for one trip where we didn't go above the legal limits. On another trip where the speedometer stayed above 75 and 80 miles per hour a good deal of the time, we saw 16.3 miles per gallon. Whipping around town produce a 13.6-mile-per-gallon average. For more than 700 miles of all types of driving, the Sting Ray averaged 14.1 miles per gallon.

A lot of this is due to the low weight the engine has to pull around, but the excellent Rochester fuel injection

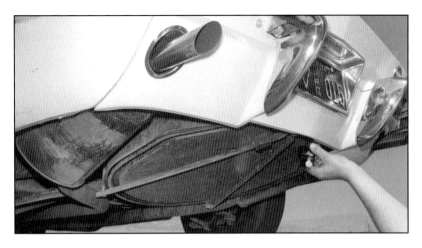

The spare location isn't as awkward as it looks, although it points up the importance of carrying overalls in the car.

A new independent rear suspension and 49/51 weight distribution require slightly different cornering techniques than before.

When viewed in profile, the aerodynamically styled Sting Ray body shows a cleanliness of line unmatched by its ancestors.

unit also has something to do with it. Like any good injection unit, it can constantly correct itself to suit different humidity, temperature, and altitude conditions. All in all, it's a completely efficient system. It doesn't seem to be temperamental, either. Care does have to be taken to keep the fuel filters clean and operating because they're quite susceptible to dirt.

We'd recommend the metallic brake option to any buyer, regardless of the engine he's getting in his new Corvette. It's very reasonably priced ($37.70) and is unmatched for efficiency. The brakes in the test car were used very hard at the end of several high-speed runs and showed very little tendency to fade. It's true that they require more pedal pressure to operate and are a trifle noisy on cold mornings, but once they get warmed up they're excellent. If a woman is going to be driving the car a lot, power assist can be added to make braking easier. Self-adjusting brakes are now standard equipment, and unlike systems in most other cars, they'll adjust as the car moves forward. The brakes in our test car pulled the Sting Ray down to quick straight-line stops time and again without any sudden locking of the wheels and without apparent fade. Several stretches of mountain roads showed that they could stand up to prolonged hard use without failure.

For all-out competition there's a special performance brake option that includes a little more effective brake lining area, bigger finned drums, power assist, and a divided output master cylinder (separate system for front and rear), and provisions for cooling. Combined with the optional cast-alloy wheels, this setup gives the competition Corvette braking power on par with many of its disc-braked competitors.

Since we had a complete analysis of the new suspension system in an earlier

All the necessary instruments are included in a well-grouped layout. The shift lever is easy to reach and the linkage has strong and positive action.

The storage area is surprisingly adequate, though some would prefer a rear opening for easier access. In a pinch, an adult can sit here on a short hop.

On a straight acceleration basis, there's very little difference between last year's car and the new one. Our quarter-mile times are within fractions of what they were last year. The only real difference is that the new one doesn't have quite the wheelspin (with stock tires) that the old rigid-axle car had.

Disappearing headlights are shown in three stages. Actuated by electric motors, they allow the Sting Ray a wind-cheating frontal design.

issue, we won't go into the theory of it here. In practice, it's far in advance, both in ride and handling, of anything now being built in the United States. It's completely comfortable without being mushy, and it takes a large chuck hole to induce any degree of harshness into the ride. Sudden dips, when taken at speed, don't produce any unpleasant oscillations, and the front and rear suspension is very hard to bottom. There's very little pitch noticeable in the ride, even though the 'Vette is built on a fairly short (98-inch) wheelbase. At high cruising speeds—and even at maximum speeds—nothing but an all-out competition car will equal it in stability. We drove it under some pretty windy conditions and didn't notice any adverse effects from crosswind loading.

We thought the old model cornered darn well, but there's no comparing it to this new one. It does take a little different technique, but once the driver gets onto it, it's beautiful. Since the 49/51 percent front-to-rear weight distribution, plus the independent rear suspension, gives the Sting Ray an inherent amount of oversteer, the driver will find that on fast corners the car will be doing most of the work through the corner instead of him powering it through.

At most speeds the coupe and the roadster are quite noisy. In addition to high engine and wind noise levels, the coupe picks up and amplifies quite a bit of road noise through the differential, which is rigidly mounted (although in rubber) to the frame. The extremely stiff ladder frame and well-designed body, with its built-in steel bracing (on the coupe), keep body shake to an absolute minimum.

The Sting Ray is roomier than the older models, and quite a bit of luggage can be carried in the space provided. Some people will be unhappy without a

CORVETTE STING RAY

2-passenger coupe

OPTIONS ON CAR TESTED: 360-horsepower fuel injection engine, 4-speed transmission, Positraction rear axle, sintered-iron brake lining, power windows, radio, whitewalls
BASIC PRICE: $4,393.75
PRICE AS TESTED: $5,321.70 (plus tax and license)
ODOMETER READING AT START OF TEST: 4,012 miles
RECOMMENDED ENGINE RED LINE: 6,500 rpm

PERFORMANCE
ACCELERATION (2 aboard)

0–30 mph	2.9 sec.
0–45 mph	4.2 sec.
0–60 mph	5.8 sec,

Standing start quarter-mile 14.5 sec. and 102 mph
Speeds in gears @ 6,500 rpm

1st . . . . 65 mph		3rd . . . . .110 mph	
2nd	88 mph	4th	130 (actual) @ 6,000 rpm

Speedometer Error on Test Car

Car's speedometer reading . . . . .30 . .45 . .51 . .61 . .72 . . .82
Weston electric speedometer . . .30 . .45 . .50 . .60 . .70 . . .80
Observed mph per 1,000 rpm in top gear 21
Stopping Distances – from 30 mph, 30 ft.; from 60 mph, 134 ft.

SPECIFICATIONS FROM MANUFACTURER
Engine
OHV V-8
Bore: 4.00 in.
Stroke: 3.25 in.
Displacement: 327 ci
Compression ratio: 11.25:1
Horsepower: 360 @ 6,000 rpm
Torque: 352 ft-lb @ 4,000 rpm
HP per CI: 1.1
Ignition: 12-volt coil

Gearbox:
4-speed, close-ratio manual; floor shift

Driveshaft
One piece—open tube

Differential
Hypoid—semi-floating (Positraction)
Standard ratio: 3.70:1

Suspension
Front: Independent, with coil springs, unequal-length upper and lower control arms direct-acting tubular shocks, and anti-roll bar
Rear: Independent, with fixed differential, transverse, nine-leaf spring, lateral struts and universally jointed axle shafts, radius arms, and direct-acting tubular shocks

Steering
Recirculating ball
Turns: 3.4 or 2.92 lock-to-lock

Wheels and Tires
5-lug, steel disc wheels
6.70 x 15 4-ply nylon tubeless tires

Brakes
Hydraulic, duo-servo, self-adjusting, with sintererd-iron linings, cast-iron drums
Front: 11-in. dia. x 2.75 in. wide
Rear: 11-in. dia. x 2.0 in. wide
Effective lining area: 134.9 sq. in.

Body and Frame
Full-length, ladder-type frame, with five crossmembers and separate body
Wheelbase: 98.0 in.
Track: front, 56.3 in.; rear, 57.0 in.
Overall length: 175.3 in.
Curb weight: 3,150 lbs.

deck lid, but it's really not too inconvenient to get to the storage space through the passenger compartment. The steering wheel is now adjustable, although not readily so from the driver's seat. It has to be done in the engine compartment with a simple wrench, but gives up to three inches of fore and aft adjustment.

The bucket seats offer more of a contour fit to the back and are very comfortable once you get used to the low seating position. A full array of instruments is functionally arranged on the dash within easy view of the driver's eyes. But their design is such that at night, with the instrument lights on, they're hard to read. The brushed aluminum backing of each gauge tends to glare. The rear window on the coupe is designed more for looks than practicality, and any decent view to the rear will have to be through an exterior side-view mirror.

CORVETTE STING RAY ROAD TEST

BOB MCVAY
Motor Trend, April 1965

*America's only true sports car performs even more precisely
with discs all around*

UNIQUE ON THE DETROIT scene—that's still Chevrolet's Corvette Sting Ray. It's as yet the only true American sports car. It makes no concessions for carrying more than two people and a reasonable amount of luggage, and it doesn't claim to be anything except what it is.

Well, what is the Corvette? It's one of the hottest-performing, best-handling, most comfortable sports cars on the market, and some think it's one of the best looking as well. Each year since its 1953 introduction, the 'Vette has been getting more refined, faster, better handling, and gentler riding.

This evolutionary change has made the Corvette easier to live with, but it didn't help out its stopping problem. The drum-brake setup just didn't keep pace with the car's sky-rocketing performance—until 1965, that is. Disc brakes are big news on the automotive scene this year, but Chevrolet's Corvette builders don't believe in doing things halfway.

All four wheels sport big, 11.75-inch-diameter disc brakes. After more than 1,500 miles behind the wheel (from slow city traffic to 124-mile-per-hour speeds on the race-track), we've formed a pretty good opinion of these stoppers. They're just great—the final component that gives an already good sports car stopping power to match its go power.

The new caliper discs use ventilated ribs. Four hydraulic pistons at each wheel press the organic linings against the discs and maintain a slight constant contact that keeps the disc wiped clean when driving in rain or under extremely dusty conditions. The amount of braking effort at the wheels is in direct proportion to the pedal effort. With four pistons per wheel (for a total of 16), plus a pedal ratio of 4.54:1, the overall ratio is 196.4:1 or about that of a conventional duo-servo drum-brake setup. But the new Corvette disc system has a much better feel and gives the driver a closer relationship to his car. Wheel lockup is much easier to predict and avoid with this system.

Inside the rear disc brakes, Chevrolet has incorporated small, 6.5-inch-diameter drum brakes with 1.75-inch-wide conventional brake shoes. These serve as the parking brake.

The splash shields, the finned discs themselves, and even the wheel and wheel covers are designed to help cool the brakes. Judging from the system's performance, they do an excellent job. Our test car came with the power (vacuum) option. This includes a dual-circuit master cylinder with separate front and rear hydraulic circuits.

In addition to our regular brake-testing procedures, we subjected the Corvette to five consecutive panic stops from 60 miles per hour—without giving the brakes any chance to cool. All stops were swerve-free, fade-free, and the wheels didn't lock up. Our shortest stop was 137 feet and the longest was 166 feet, for a 153.65-foot average stopping distance for our five stops. It felt as if the brakes could continue to perform this way all day long.

We also used the brakes hard on long, fast, winding, downhill mountain roads, in city traffic, and during one of Los Angeles' infamous cloudbursts. After 1,500 miles, in our opinion, the 1965 Corvette has the finest, smoothest-acting, and strongest set of stoppers available on any American automobile.

A fully independent suspension provided excellent traction on the road, off the road, and on the track. The car showed minimum of lean and understeer and maximum control at speed.

Important though they are, brakes are only one component of many that go into building a sports car. Suspension is also very important, and here's where the Corvette shines again with a refined, fully independent system. They've shifted more weight to the rear for better traction this year. Distribution is approximately 47/53. A five-crossmember frame mounts the 31-piece convertible body at four points on rubber biscuits, while the coupe body attaches to the frame at six points.

Independent, variable-rate coils up front (with a .687-inch-diameter anti-roll bar) are standard. A .94-inch-diameter bar comes with the stiffer suspension option. A nine-element, transverse-leaf, variable-rate spring is mounted at the rear, with strut rods and torque control arms. Direct double-acting shocks, with special freon-filled bags inside, are used at each corner.

This car was definitely built with fast, safe driving in mind. It should prove, in the hands of an experienced driver, to be one of the quickest in captivity. At low speeds around town or on rough roads, ride is a bit choppy, but the Corvette is far more comfortable and easy to live with than many other sports cars. As speed increases, so does

The roadster shows versatility, with three distinctive body styles when the optional hardtop is ordered. Taking off the top can be a chore and is definitely not a one-person job. Once in place, the top rattled and required lots of muscle to lift up in order to get into the luggage compartment.

riding comfort. For high-speed travel over any kind of road, it'll be hard to find a more comfortable sports car.

The Sting Ray feels almost perfectly neutral in corners until pushed right to the limit. At that point, there's some understeer and subsequent carb flooding. But the Corvette can be cornered fast and flat on the track or on the road. Once set into a bend, we found that only slight changes in the throttle setting could alter our course, without our moving the

Proving its mettle on California's winding mountain roads, our Corvette proved itself a fast, controllable sports car that was comfortable, quiet, and a joy to drive and live with.

2-door, 2-passenger convertible

OPTIONS ON CAR TESTED: 300-horsepower V-8, 4-speed manual transmission, Positraction, power brakes-steering-windows, removable fiberglass hardtop, AM-FM radio, power antenna, tinted glass, whitewalls.
BASE PRICE: $4,106
PRICE AS TESTED: $5,279.35 (plus tax and license)
ODOMETER READING AT START OF TEST: 2,000 miles
RECOMMENDED ENGINE RED LINE: 5,500 rpm

PERFORMANCE
ACCELERATION (2 aboard)

0–30 mph	3.1 sec.
0–45 mph	4.6 sec.
0–60 mph	7.5 sec.

PASSING TIMES AND DISTANCES

40–60 mph	4.1 sec., 299.3 ft.
50–70 mph	4.3 sec., 378.4 ft.

Standing start quarter-mile 15.8 sec. and 90 mph
Speeds in gears @ 5,500 rpm

1st	50 mph	3rd	90 mph
2nd	70 mph	4th	124 mph

@ 5,200 rpm (observed)
Speedometer Error on Test Car
 Car's speedometer reading . . . . .30 . .45 . .51 . .61 . .71 . .81
 Weston electric speedometer . . .30 . .45 . .50 . .60 . .70 . .80
Observed miles per hour per 1,000 rpm in top gear . . . . . .23 mph
Stopping Distances—from 30 mph, 30.5 ft.; from 60 mph, 137.0 ft.

SPECIFICATIONS FROM MANUFACTURER
Engine
 OHV V-8
 Bore: 4.00 in.
 Stroke: 3.25 in.
 Displacement: 327 ci
 Compression ratio: 10.5:1
 HP: 300 @ 5,000 rpm
 HP per ci: 0.92
 Torque: 350 ft-lb @ 4,000 rpm
 Carburetion: 1 4-barrel
 Ignition: 12-volt coil

Gearbox
 4-speed manual, all-synchro, with reverse lock-out; floorshift
Driveshaft
 1-piece, open tube

Differential
 Hypoid, semi-floating (Positraction)
 Standard ratio: 3.36:1

Suspension
 Front: Independent, with coil springs, unequal-length upper and lower control arms, direct-acting tubular shocks, and anti-roll bar
 Rear: Independent, with fixed differential, transverse, nine-leaf springs, lateral struts, and universally jointed axle shafts, radius arms, and direct-acting tubular shocks

Steering
 Semi-reversible recirculating ball nut; linkage-type power assist
 Turning diameter: 39.9 ft.
 Turns lock-to-lock: 3.4 or 2.92 (optional)

Wheels and Tires
 5-lug, steel, short-spoke spider wheels
 7.75x15 4-ply tubeless rayon whitewall tires

Brakes
 Hydraulic 4-wheel caliper discs with integral power assist and dual-circuit master cylinders
 Front: 11.75-in. dia x 4 hydraulic pistons & 2 shoes per disc
 Rear: 11.75-in. dia., with 6.5-in. dia. x 1.75 in. wide drums for parking brake
 Effective lining area: 83.4 sq. in.
 Swept disc area: 461.2 sq. in.

Body and Frame
 31-panel fiberglass body, attached to welded steel, ladder-type frame
 Wheelbase: 98.0 in.
 Track: front, 56.8 in.; rear, 57.6 in.
 Overall length: 175.1 in.
 Overall width: 69.6 in.
 Overall height: 49.8 in.
 Curb weight: 3,280 lbs.

wheel. But at all times, we had a feeling of complete control. The Corvette could be drifted, skidded, or just driven very fast through any variety of turns with a high degree of safety and control. It's a car that a good driver can really fall in love with, and one that a bad driver, or an over-enthusiastic one, can get himself into trouble with just as quickly.

Positraction was a big help in preventing wheelspin in corners, during acceleration, and especially on wet pavement. With power steering and brakes on our test car, control meant a very light touch. The rear felt just a bit twitchy on wet or dirt roads, but once we got the feel of the car, it proved able to do anything we asked.

The 300-horsepower or the standard 250-horsepower version of the Corvette's multi-horsepower 327-ci V-8 won't make anyone a king at the local drag strip. But you can rest

First you have to know the procedure, then the top goes up or down with ease. The louvers and wheel covers are new this year.

Six acrylic lacquer finishes and a combination of interior tones give buyers a wide color choice. Convertible tops come in black, white, and beige.

assured that if you aren't satisfied beating most of the people most of the time, you can always order a hotter version. The 350-horsepower "street" version and a 365-horsepower option top off the carburetor-mounted engines, while fuel injection injects a fire-breathing 375 horsepower into this fiberglass beauty. And that one ought to be fast enough for anyone. If it isn't, just wait for the 396-inch V-8 soon to be introduced.

Inside the Corvette, there's a very functional dashboard, with big, legible gauges. Everything's within easy reach, especially that beautifully smooth, precise, four-speed transmission and its handy, short chrome lever.

Six acrylic lacquer finishes and a combination of interior tones give buyers a wide color choice. Convertible tops come in black, white, and beige. And there's a coupe body, too. New seats for 1965 give more lateral support during hard cornering plus somewhat better support than last year's seats. New molded door panels boast integral armrests.

Our "commuter" Corvette, with its 300-horsepower engine, was a very easy car to live with—much more so than former fuel injection models we've driven. It started easily, was completely docile in traffic, needed only first and fourth for most normal demands, and it was very quiet. On the other hand, it gave excellent performance for a 3,280-pound car when we used the 5,500 rpm redline and the four-speed gearbox to the fullest extent.

Most normal driving gave between 11 and 14 miles per gallon of premium gas, but steady highway cruising boosted this up to around 17 miles per gallon with the standard 3.36 rear axle. Optional axles range from 3.08 to 4.56.

In standard form, Corvette's 1965 offerings are smooth, quiet, comfortable sports cars, capable of staggering performance depending on what engine you order. A better all-around sports car would be hard to find at any price. Here's a car a man can really enjoy driving and living with. We loved it.

SURVIVOR 'VETTE

TONY SWAN
Motor Trend, December 1976

When it comes to L-88s, old doesn't necessarily mean feeble

IT CAME FROM THE FACTORY with something called the C-48 option listed on the invoice. But when you checked into the C-48 option, one of the first things you learned was that you were optioning to leave things *off*—the heater and defroster, for example—in the interest of weight saving and keeping the thing off public roads.

What manner of car was this L-88 C-48 Corvette Stingray? Just this: your basic right off the assembly line ready-to-go road racer, complete with trick suspension, heavy-duty close-ratio gearbox, and 560 horsepower.

Conceived by Corvette genius Zora Arkus-Duntov as a logical step in the 'Vette's evolution as a no-holds-barred street racer, it wound up being a high water mark for American production and semi-production engines, the last brute roar before the strangulation of the emissions regulations.

Not many of them left the factory. Chevrolet, which maintained a low profile in all its racing activities, never published horsepower figures of any kind for the engine and production statistics on the L-88s were sketchy. According to statistics produced by a member of the Corvette merchandising staff, there were 20 C-48s produced, 16 of them with the aluminum head engines that snorted out so much raw power.

In an effort to whittle something off the weight differential between the high-performance 427 L-88 and the old small-block Chevy engines, Duntov used aluminum components wherever possible: the heads (which represented a savings of 75 pounds over the cast iron heads); the forged aluminum pop-up pistons; the intake manifold, designed to form a plenum chamber under the single four-barrel Holley 850 CFM carburetor; an aluminum water pump; and an aluminum cross-flow radiator.

The block for the racing setup was the same as Chevrolet's other 427s, but there were some internal differences, such as the forged steel crankshaft, which was cross-drilled and Tufftrided, and the main bearing caps, secured by four bolts rather than two. The valves featured triple springs, pushrods with specially hardened ends, and heat-treated rocker

The L-88 C-48 Corvette Stingray was a ready-to-go racer right off the assembly line. It came complete with trick suspension, a heavy-duty close-ratio gearbox, and 560 horsepower.

arms, the latter another touch unique to these engines.

The L-88 connecting rods were shot-peened and fastened with extra-strong .716-inch bolts.

Compression was a hefty 12.5:1, and peak performance was achieved with 103 octane gasoline.

Innovation didn't stop with the engine's hardware. Chevrolet included its then-new K-66 electronic ignition as part of the L-88 package, to make sure the spark was hot enough to match the rest of the setup.

The no-compromise approach continued behind the bellhousing with a heavy-duty clutch and Corvette's M-22 Muncie four-speed transmission, an option available to all 'Vette buyers in 1966 but sold only with the L-88 C-48 package in 1967. The close-ratio box featured reduced helix angle gearing for extra strength, to deal with the L-88's out-wrenching torque and power. The transmission distinguished itself in combat but was so noisy that Corvette engineers nicknamed it "the rock crusher."

Three other factory performance packages were included with the L-88 C-48: the G-80 limited slip differential, in either 3.70:1 or 4.11:1 ratios; the J-56 four-wheel disc brake setup, utilizing rayon reinforced brake hoses, wrought nickel alloy backing plates, and metallic heat-resistant brake pads; and a suspension package—F-41—that was heavy-duty all around. Included under the latter heading were extra-stiff coils up front, double-strength leaf springs in the rear, extra-large shocks, and an extra-heavy anti-roll bar in front. The F-41 suspension sat about 1½ inches lower than the stock 1967 Corvette.

The setup was clearly intended to go fast and that's exactly what it did. The aluminum head version of the L-88 was first raced in prototype form, wearing Sunoco colors with Roger Penske listed as entrant, in the 1966 Daytona and Sebring endurance races, where it took GT honors in both events. Dick Guldstrand, George Wintersteen, and Ben Moore drove to 12th overall at Daytona, and Wintersteen and Moore piloted the car to ninth overall at Sebring.

The following year the L-88 C-48 option was made available on production Corvettes, and four of them made an assault on Sebring. One, driven by Don Yenko and Dave Morgan, wound up tops in GT and tenth overall even though it spent the last 40 minutes of the race wedged in a sandbank after the brakes went away.

However, the most awesome speed achievement of a road racing L-88 came later that same year, when Dana Chevrolet of California, with sub-rosa factory encouragement, entered a 'Vette in the Le Mans 24-hour classic. Although the car was hardly a wraith at 3,200-pounds-plus—reportedly some 300 pounds heavier than anything in the race—it was by far the fastest thing in the GT field that year. With Guldstrand and Bob

Bondurant splitting the driving, the 'Vette went some 20 miles per hour faster than any Corvette had ever gone, hitting 171.5 miles per hour on the Mulsanne straight before breaking its engine 11½ hours into the race. The top speed was 22 miles per hour faster than the Ferrari that took GT honors in the race.

Instrumented performance data on these precious L-88s was hard to come by. Naturally, there weren't many of them around for the edification and amusement of the motoring press back in 1967, but you could get a somewhat tamer version of the 'Vette for street terrorization. This was the 427 Tri-Power setup, a triple-carbureted growler with iron block and heads that pumped out 435 horsepower at 5,800 rpm and a whopping 460 ft-lb of torque at 4,000 rpm.

Motor Trend was able to lay hands on a 427 Tri-Power Stingray back in '67 and obtained the following test results: 0–30, 2.5 seconds; 0–60, 5.5 seconds; quarter-mile, 13.8 seconds, 104 miles per hour; top speed, 143 miles per hour at 6,000 rpm. These numbers fall a trifle short of the L-88's off-the-shelf potential but were pretty hairy on their own, particularly when contrasted with today's whipped cream GTs.

All race cars have the life expectancy of a demolitions man with a bad case of the shakes: short. Of the 16 aluminum head L-88s that rolled out to do battle in 1967, only three survive today, so far as we know. And the one you see pictured here might very well have joined its ancestors at the big Corvette track in the sky had it not been for the ministrations of Jim Whitmore, who discovered it behind a gas station in Hugoton, Kansas.

Whitmore is an affable Oklahoma City Corvette addict whose work as an insurance safety inspector takes him to lots of backwaters where he's able to pursue his hobby, which he defines as "rattin' up all kinds of old Corvette engines and parts."

Driving this muscle-bound relic from the golden age of go is a revelation, particularly for the visitor who has just stepped out of a fresh-from-the-factory '77 Corvette.

The '67 coupe he found in Hugoton looked appropriately ratty.

"It looked just terrible," Whitmore recalled. "The rear end was all broken, someone had put eight-inch fender flares on it and done a flame job with a paint-brush. There was a big spoiler on the back and the 427 was gone; someone stuck a 283 into it. I got it for $800."

At that point, Whitmore assumed he was facing just another Corvette fixup project—his ninth or tenth.

"It was my brother who discovered what I had, really," he said. "It seemed a little odd to me that there was no radio or heater, but I didn't think too much about it at first. Then we got it all apart and discovered the metal brake pads. The kid who sold it to me told me he'd bought it from some guy who trailered it and only drove it in races, and there were only 21,000 miles on the clock. My brother remembered reading something about the L-88s somewhere once, and we began trying to get more information about the cars."

The next clue was the noisy "rock crusher" M-22 transmission, which a Corvette merchandiser was able to verify as OEM only with the C-48 package. The K-66 ignition, still on board and in working order, and L-41 suspension confirmed the suspicions of the brothers Whitmore. Jim had stumbled onto some sort of rare survivor 'Vette, and he set about restoring it to some semblance of its former potential.

He began by getting hold of a 427 engine in another Corvette, swapping it for the 283 in his C-48 and selling the leftovers.

"Then I ratted up all the aluminum goodies for the 427," he said. "And I was lucky— I found a set of heads with the valves in and everything okay. I had to swap a *big* pile of parts for 'em."

When Whitmore had pried loose the spoiler and fender flares and scraped down through several layers of paint and patching, he found more evidence of a racing history.

"I'm pretty sure the car's been up against guardrails a few times," he said. "Three of the four corners have been crunched one time or another, it's had at least one new front end, and it may have been flipped, although I'm not sure about that."

On the outside, the car now looks almost as good as the day it left St. Louis. But under the hood, Whitmore's been forced to make some compromises with the realities of low-budget restoration. The pistons are garden variety flat-topped; Whitmore was obliged to get compression down somewhat, since 103 octane gas is about as plentiful as surplus zeppelins in today's world of motorsports. The K-66 ignition was also discarded when Whitmore found his spark plugs were lasting "about four hours a set." Not only was it expensive and inconvenient to replace plugs every other outing, there was also the risk of stripping threads out of one of those aluminum heads. Whitmore substituted a dual-point Accel ignition system. For smoother performance at low rpm, Whitmore substituted a

780 CFM Holley four-barrle carb for the original 850 CFM. The original aluminum radiator was gone when Whitmore found the car, and he hasn't been able to "rat up" another one.

There have been changes outside the engine compartment as well. In order to keep his rig competitive at the autocrosses, Whitmore has installed eight-inch rims in favor of the OEM six-inch ones, and, by using spring risers, he's raised the body back to standard 1967 height to accommodate bigger tires. Standard Corvette fiber brake pads have been adapted to the J-56 calipers, since the metal pads take too long to get up to operating temperature and are noisy besides. And to make the package sound even sweeter, glasspack mufflers have been substituted for the original low-restriction factory mufflers.

"Those factory mufflers were the worst sounding I've ever heard," he said. "Just didn't sound like a Chevy."

Driving this muscle-bound relic from the golden age of go is a revelation, particularly for the visitor who has just stepped out of a fresh-from-the-factory '77 Corvette. Out of respect for the age of his machine, which was never noted for reliability even in its youth, Whitmore uses a 5,000 rpm redline, but this is hardly a restriction at all. The L-88 will break its tires loose at almost any speed in the first three gears, and easily enough in fourth gear as well.

The initial impression is of early Can Am brute horsepower, of course. No question about it; this thing will flat throw back its head and howl when you stamp on it. Even with his detunings and improvisations, Whitmore still figures he's getting well over 430 horsepower. But a prompt secondary impression is the amazing manageability of all that horsepower. Aside from the very low rpm ranges, the engine exhibits excellent throttle response and smooth acceleration, revving quite willingly up to redline through all the gears, thanks to the close-ratio gearbox (which whines in a reassuringly truck-like manner).

And the handling qualities are straight from the track. Body roll is very limited, and the car responds sensitively to throttle steering. It's a package of surprising subtlety considering its horsepower credentials and velocity heritage (such as 170 miles per hour-plus at Le Mans). It's a real thrill to grab hold of the big steering wheel, which has almost no rake at all, thanks to its proximity to the dashboard, and hurl this veteran around a slalom course. Even if you're not fast it sure as hell *sounds* and *feels* like you're fast.

Whitmore, who prefers autocrossing to drag racing, hasn't done much in the quarter-mile with his car. But even with his self-imposed redline and a disinclination to subject the L-88 to the tortures of all-out acceleration, he's turned quarters in the high 13s.

"But this isn't the fastest one around," he said. "There are guys coming to meets now with 494s and 510s; you can still get a 510 short block from Chevy. Some guy down in Dallas has a setup similar to mine with a 510 and he's running low 11s.

"I guess I'm getting ready for my next one, really. I can't really enjoy racing this one anymore because it's too valuable; I find myself waiting for it to break."

Accordingly, Whitmore plans to pass his dinosaur along to another keeper. We just hope the L-88 finds as good a home as it did in Oklahoma City.

SPORTS CAR TOURNAMENT: COBRA vs. CORVETTE

STEVE KELLY
Motor Trend, March 1968

Comparison shows the Shelby car has much to do before overwhelming the well-established 'Vette

JUST ON A SUBJECTIVE BASIS, comparison between these two is scant. Appearance is vastly different, and on that basis alone, there'd be no stacking them against one another. But they do hit "head on" in the marketplace, and no matter how much either maker likes or dislikes it, they have to meet somewhere. If not in the showroom, then it might as well be here.

The Cobra costs less. Very few options are listed, so a full-list Cobra adds up to fewer dollars than a full-list Corvette with near-comparable equipment. Resale value may show a higher rate of depreciation, and the Corvette has more in the way of standard equipment goodies. Things like lamp-monitors, four-wheel disc brakes, flow-through ventilation, forward opening hood, and independent rear suspension are standard Corvette items not even available for the Cobra.

Maintenance will show up as being less on a 428 Cobra than a 427 Corvette. This applies to only the biggest-engined cars, and based on the smallest-engined versions, it is about a draw. The Cobra, using the Mustang for a birthplace, is more readily acceptable in the average garage, but anyone who kicks out $4,500 or so for any car isn't going to trust the "average" garage for service. He'll go to a specialist, where he will most likely find a Corvette. A draw here, too.

Insurance rates are way over in the Cobra's favor. Being mostly steel, body repair costs are significantly lower than for the 'glass Corvette. There's also a reputation factor involved. In its 16-year life, 'Vettes have managed to become unwanted merchandise around many insurance offices. The feeling is—and justifiably so in lots of cases—that the Corvette driver is more likely to become engaged in an accident than if he were driving a more domesticated vehicle.

More people can fit in the Cobra, but judging from letters submitted in response to our '67 article comparing the two, not many people care. About the last thing either car is bought for is carrying the gang around town. Luggage though, is a more acceptable item in the Cobra. The small space behind the Corvette seats will take one or two suitcases, while the trunk and rear seat of the Cobra can hold many more.

Comfort-wise, the Corvette is nicer for drive. The seats don't wear you out on a long trip, nor give you bad aches where they most hurt. Entry and exit are easier in the Cobra since it's higher.

To park the Corvette takes some expertise in deciding where the nose ends. It drops down out of sight long before it ends. This problem exists to a much lesser degree in the Cobra.

True handling and acceleration are best handled by the Corvette. The wide-pattern tires (new, optionally for '68) make it superior to anything made in quantity production in the United States. And that 427 "rat motor" is an engine that has left every other maker envious. Of course, a Mopar Hemi 426 seems to get the job done a bit better, but at more cost, and besides, you can't get it in the Cobra.

The comparison is here, and in a good number of instances, it is straight across. Each has good and bad points, and each has distinctiveness all its own.

COBRA

One of our office experts claims Shelby-American's last "good" Mustang-based car was the '66. We go along with him—almost. The '66 was much more of a sports car than the '67 and '68, but finding a market for it was harder. Performance was there for the real hard-core rough-riding enthusiast, but their number is vastly overwhelmed by the buying group preferring both power and comfort. For Shelby-American and Ford's sake, the last two years have proved better cars, sales and acceptance being the criteria.

In a sense, Shelby has sold out to the add-on and chrome-it establishment. The new cars are more decorated than the old and show strains of having too much ornamentation. The convertible model seems especially so, with too many lines going too many ways.

427 Corvette

428 Cobra

Because of the now historic Ford assembly-line strike, we were only able to obtain a GT 500 for instrumented testing. However, at the preview last summer of '68 Shelby products, we lived with the GT 350, 302-ci V-8–powered car for a brief session. It lacks substantially in power when compared to its earlier mates, but then has less horsepower. A hydraulic cam and cast-iron exhaust manifolds are used, and they tend to tame the power and noise. It is many degrees quieter than the old 306-horsepower "street" combination on '67s, but is likely to please more than it will offend by this virtue.

Shelby-American has sold out to the "chrome-it" and "add-on" establishment. The Mustang interior has been added to but not improved. Imitation mag wheel covers add final, phony touch.

Our GT 500 convertible came with the standard 428-ci V-8 and endeared itself to us by exhibiting calm behavior. It likes to eat gas, but otherwise seems no different from a 390-ci Mustang. Performance is substantially better than a 390, but not as much as you'd expect. This is more of an engine for "I want power" advocates than anything else. We doubt it'll beat any 427 Corvette for acceleration, and it falls in a bad class for drag racing, per NHRA specs. The size puts it out of contention for sedan racing, so the 428 is relegated to street duties primarily. At that, it is fine.

Slow speed operation isn't cause for trouble. Response from idle or sub 20-mile-per-hour speeds is quite good. We had a Cruise-O-Matic transmission in our test GT and prefer it for normal use. Shifting is crisp and happens at reasonable speeds. Kickdown is easy, and you can usually reach passing-gear at all maximum speed limits.

The gear selector is of the "sport-shift" type, making for manual control throughout. Second gear has a high-speed monitor preventing over-revving on downshifts. The driver is responsible for this on upshifts. Gear changing on full throttle runs requires a 200–300-rpm anticipation. In other words, if you want to shift at 5,500 rpm, better move the lever at 5,200.

The 428 will live at 6,000 rpm, but better times will come about shifting at 5,500. Torque is hefty enough to slip the tires between first and second, as well as from standstill.

Handling, Steering & Stopping
Suspension is less of a "springless" proposition than exhibited in '65–'66 GTs, but still firm. Relocation of the upper front control arms as was done in the early models isn't needed in the new Cobras. Expense and ride harshness rose with this move, and few people understood its value. The overall suspension is very close to Ford's own performance-handling option, yet the Shelbys have an edge. High-speed straight-line driving isn't at all abusive, and the cornering work is a safe proposition. We like cars with firm control and found this in the Shelby Cobras.

The ungainly roll bar is best kept covered by the convertible top.

Steering is right out of Mustang land. At least the feeling of "plasticity" is. Response is not at all like the Corvette's, and there just seems to be unwanted lag in the unit. The steering wheel is not up to sports car standards. We've got a good idea Shelby folks agree here, but the standard wheel meets federal specs for impact absorption and a wood-rimmed steel-spoke flat disc doesn't (such as the '67 item). It protrudes closer to the driver's chest than is comfortable, causing us to "kink" our arms even with the seat at full travel. We're not positive of the ruling for or against owner installation of the old-style wheel, but we'll bet it will be done often.

COBRA POWERTEAMS

	Displacement	Carburetion	Horsepower-Torque	Transmission
V-8 302[1]	4-barrel	250 @ 4,800 rpm	310 ft-lb @ 3,200 rpm	4-speed Cruise-O-Matic[*]
V-8 428 [2]	4-barrel	360 @ 5,400 rpm	459 ft-lb @ 3,200 rpm	4-speed Cruise-O-Matic[*]
V-8 427[*]	4-barrel	400 @ 5,600 rpm	460 ft-lb @ 3,200 rpm	4-speed Cruise-O-Matic[*]
1. Std. 6T350 engine		2. Std. GT500 engine	[*]optional	

Stopping GTs is about like stopping Corvettes; no trouble at all. The front disc/rear drum setup is power assisted, using Ford Motor Company's "floating" caliper front brake. The rear drum is revised over the standard Mustang with a 10-inch-diameter x 2¼-inch-wide drum. High-performance lining material is used.

Braking is straight, quick, and free from serious fade. Use of the Goodyear E70x15 high-speed tires contributes heavily by planting lots of rubber on the asphalt.

Comfort, Convenience & Ride

We'd like to see better front bucket seats in the Cobras. While those in use are fairly comfortable, they get tiresome after 90 minutes driving or more. They are deluxe Mustang units, with good construction but a need for more seat padding for all-out comfort. The

The seats in the Corvette are extremely comfortable, but when the driver seat is in full rear position, the safety latch is impossible to reach. The handling and steering are excellent.

The Corvette interior is well laid out; all gauges are easily visible.

seatback is too straight and could be neatly reclined a degree or two. Our test convertible had a crooked seatback and, though repairable, it is really a nuisance.

Addition of a center console to all '68 Cobras is a great idea, though decorating it with paper wood-grain applique is not. It's easily identifiable as paper and shows less class than vinyl covering. The just-right height armrest hides a huge storage bin. Because of the near-nothing capacity of Mustang glove boxes, Cobra owners really make out. If the door armrest were as comfortable as the console pad, things would really be looking good.

Rear seat entry in either coupe or convertible is worthy of study. Some prefer stooping and diving under the roll bar in the convertible and through the shoulder harnesses on the fastback. Others manage to delicately thread their way in, turn around facing forward, and then sit down contentedly. We never did set a pattern, but somehow managed the maneuver. It's not all that bad, but a long way from having the convenience of a sedan.

Ride is, of necessity, stiff. Bounce is somewhat hard, but we didn't once incur loss of rear wheel traction over hard dips. The best description might be that you know it is stiff, but nothing more. The cars handle the job of plain riding in good style. This new ride-pattern is about halfway between stock Mustang and that of the "rough rider" '66 GT.

Plus & Minus Features
It might be a good idea to further separate the fog light switch from the convertible top button. They're right next to each other, and at night, without lights, it'd be easy to rip the top right off its anchors.

Another better idea would be to soften the trunk torsion bars. After removing the stock sheet-metal panel and replacing it with fiberglass, the hinges have much less weight to carry, and consequently spring the trunk up like a flag in a shooting gallery.

That great big hatch-type hood interferes with forward vision, cutting off several feet of right-in-front sight.

The hood pins used to release the panel are neat, taking only a turn to undo them. They stay with the hood when raised so theft or loss is discounted. Functional louvers on each side allow air to escape, but we noticed the openings are right over the plug wires, with no deflectors for water being included. We louvered a hood once and put an aluminum panel below the louvers angled down and to the side of the engine compartment. If we can do it, anyone can!

Shelby's integrated roll bar idea deserves high praise. It also deserves to be copied. Any convertible is potentially more dangerous than a hardtop, and occupants' lives are worth more than an additional few dollars of tubing.

Cobra shoulder belts are the best yet. The hardtop uses suspender-type restraints, stemming from a single strap into an inertia reel harness, allowing slow body movement but locking up on sharp impact. The convertible restraint is housed in the rear quarter panel, pulling out and fitting against the front occupant's chest and fastening to a center tunnel-mounted buckle strap. The inertia reel is featured here also.

The "establishment" has had its impact on Shelby-American, and the carmakers have succumbed and resisted. Styling reflects the adoption of the "great" philosophy, but performance and safety still are Shelby's own exclusives.

CORVETTE

Getting emotionally "hung up" on the Corvette styling takes somewhat longer than becoming enthused over its great driving characteristics—but not much. Getting in and out is more of a chore than on earlier models, but like styling and ride, is only a matter of accommodating one's particular personality.

From the looks of things, it appears that Corvette assembly-line workers are taking time getting used to putting the new model together. Rough panels and ill-fitting sections, highly evident on early-run cars, indicate some practice is needed before perfection could be neared.

Our test cars were both convertibles. One came with a 327-ci, 350-horsepower V-8, the other with a 427-ci, 435-horsepower semi-hemi head engine. Compression on both is 11.0:1, and only four-speed transmissions are offered here.

The flow-through ventilation on the Corvette works, making for windows-up driving in all but the hottest weather.

Raw power is Corvette symbolism, and five different engines are available for '68 in 327- and 427-ci sizes.

The 327 engine uses a single four-barrel Rochester carb and quiet-running hydraulic cam and lifters. Lift is .4472-inch on intake and exhaust, with 306-degree opening duration on each. Valve opening overlap is 78 degrees, and valve head diameter is 2.02 inches for intake and 1.60 inches on the exhaust.

Road handling is much improved over '67 models and suspension got stiffer.

From the looks of things, it appears that Corvette assembly-line workers are taking time getting used to putting the new model together. Rough panels and ill-fitting sections, highly evident on early-run cars, indicate some practice is needed before perfection could be neared.

Noise out of the engine room doesn't herald an "over-one-horsepower-per-cubic-inch" engine lurking there. A 3.70:1 final drive gear kept our top speed down to an exacted 117.15 miles per hour at 5,500 rpm. The 0–60-mile-per-hour times and quarter-mile runs could be greatly improved by a stronger clutch and drag tires, but we weren't all that disappointed with the cars' recordings. City traffic operation was so near-perfect that we accepted the semi-compromise between "rump-rump" idling and reliability with praise. Some experimenting with tires and tuning will drop the 350-horsepower 'Vette into the mid 13-second bracket without difficulty.

The 435-horsepower test machine had Chevy's L-88 aluminum head option, and frankly we thought it'd go quicker than it did. Tuning time was shortened by inclement weather, so we had to settle for 14-second quarter-mile times. But our earlier 427 cars ('66 & '67) both hit the 13s right off the bat. The '68 in proper tune should be high 12s. The majority of drag-strip disciplined Corvettes hit the low 12-second mark, with a good many in the 11-second bracket. The potential is undoubtedly there.

We encountered trouble getting the triple carburetion to work in unison. Several times, the front and rear Holley two-barrels refused to work. Some jerry-rigging on the vacuum linkage helps, but there's no substitute for mechanical actuation—available at most speed or specialty shops.

This big engine objects to long idling periods, but cleans out quickly once on the move, with only a small amount of plug fouling. Clutch action is stiff, allowing the driver to object to idling time also. The throw is much shorter than on the 350-horsepower engine, negating much worry about the pedal hanging-up between power shifts.

Solid lifters are used on all 435-horsepower engines. Valve diameter is 2.190-inch intake and 1.720-inch exhaust. Lift is .5197-inch on both, intake opening duration is 316 degrees and exhaust is 302 degrees with overlap being 80 degrees.

CORVETTE POWERTEAMS					
1. Std. GT350 engine			2. Std. GT500 engine		*optional
V-8	327	4-barrel	300 @ 5,000 rpm	360 ft-lb @ 3,400 rpm	3-speed
					4-speed* Turbo Hydra-Matic
V-8	327*	4-barrel	350 @ 5,800 rpm	360 ft-lb @ 3,600 rpm	4-speed* (close or wide ratio)
V-8	427*	4-barrel	390 @ 5,400 rpm	460 ft-lb @ 3,600 rpm	4-speed* (close or wide ratio)
					Turbo Hydra-Matic
V-8	427*	3 2-barrel	400 @ 5,400 rpm	460 ft-lb @ 3,600 rpm	4-speed* (close or wide ratio)
					Turbo Hydra-Matic

Handling, Steering & Stopping

Handling, both on twisting roads and straight-arrow stretches is improved over '67 by at least 100 percent. Introduction of wide-pattern tires—7-inch-wide wheels—as standard gets most of the credit. Also making big contributions are the reduced height (approx. 2 inches) and wider rear track (.7-inch). Terming it a truly stable road car is far from exaggeration.

Manual and power steering units are quick to react. Power can't be had with the 435-horsepower engine, but we didn't mind. Only 3.4 turns of the 16-inch-diameter wheel takes it from lock-to-lock, and only 2.92 are needed with power. Overall ratio on manual is 20.2:1 and 17.6:1 with power. Suspension feedback and/or sloppiness is not a problem here. It just doesn't exist.

Understeer is fairly inherent, but constant adjusting of the wheel isn't required while rounding curves. Once set—it stays. Oversteer is only a problem, or condition, encountered with the rear end braking loose.

Since '65, poor stopping Corvettes haven't been produced. With disc brakes at all four corners, they just plant themselves to the ground and come to rest straight and quick. Less than 120 feet from 60 to 0 miles per hour (a distance we repeatedly accomplished) is something to write home about.

The 'Vette's four-wheel disc brakes remind us of the auto company spokesman who recently defended his company's nonuse of them by explaining difficulties in adapting a suitable parking brake to the system. Hmm? Wonder how Mercedes, Porsche, Volvo, Chevrolet, etc. did it? Gee!

Comfort, Convenience & Ride

Stetson wearers will find ample space for their headgear—behind the front seat. Rooflines are low, negating hat wearing.

PERFORMANCE

	Cobra 428	Corvette 327	Corvette 427
Acceleration (2 aboard)			
0–30 mph	3.0 sec.	3.2 sec.	2.7 sec.
0–45 mph	4.3 sec.	4.8 sec.	4.0 sec.
0–60 mph	6.5 sec.	7.1 sec.	6.3 sec.
0–75 mph	9.4 sec.	10.0 sec.	8.3 sec.
Passing speeds			
40–60 mph	2.5 sec. 183.0 ft.	3.1 sec. 227 ft.	2.7 sec. 197 ft.
50–70 mph	3.0 sec. 264 ft.	3.6 sec. 316 ft.	2.9 sec. 255 ft.
Standing start			
Quarter-mile	14.75 sec. 98 mph	15.0 sec. 92 mph	14.1 sec. 103 mph
Speeds in gears			
1st ...mph @ rpm	47 @ 5,500	53 @ 5,500	66 @ 6,500
2nd...	79 @ 5,500	71 @ 5,500	88 @ 6,500
3rd...	116 @ 5,500	92 @ 5,500	116 @ 6,500
4th...		117 @ 5,500	160 @ 6,500
Mph per 1,000 @ rpm	21.1	21.2	24.7
Stopping distances			
from 30 mph	39 ft.	27 ft.	29 ft.
from 60 mph	151 ft.	117 ft.	119 ft.
Speedometer error			
at 60 mph	5% fast	6% fast	none
Mileage range	9.0–15.0 mpg	10.6–20.0 mpg	7.8–17.5 mpg
Average mileage	12.8 mpg	15.7 mpg	13.6 mpg

TEST CAR SPECIFICATIONS

	Cobra 428	Corvette 327	Corvette 427
Engine	OHV V-8	OHV V-8	OHV V-8
Bore x stroke	4.13 x 3.984 in.	4.0 x 3.25 in.	4.25 x 3.76 in.
Displacement, ci	428	327	427
Hp @ rpm	360 @ 5,400	350 @ 5,800	435 @ 5,800
Torque, ft-lb @ rpm	459 @ 3,200	360 @ 3,600	460 @ 4,000
Compression ratio	10.5:1	11.0:1	11.0:1
Carburetion	1 4-barrel	1 4-barrel	3 2-barrel
Transmission	Automatic; 3-speed	Manual; 4-speed	Manual; 4-speed
Final drive ratio	3.50:1	3.70:1	3.55:1
Steering	Recirculating ball & nut w/power assist	Recirculating ball & nut w/power	Recirculating ball & nut Manual
Overall steering ratio	2.03	17.6:1	20.2:1
Turning dia., curb-to-curb	39.4 ft.	39.9 ft.	39.9 ft.
Wheel turns, lock-to-lock	3.6	2.92	3.4
Tires	E70 x 15 high-speed	F70 x 15	F70 x 15
Brakes	front disc/ rear drum with power assist	4-wheel disc with integral power	4-wheel disc with integral power
Fuel capacity	17 gal.	20 gal.	20 gal.
Curb weight, lbs.	3,665	3,445	3,425
Body frame construction	Steel unit	Ladder frame	Ladder frame
Wheelbase, ins.	108	98	98
Front track, ins.	58.1	58.3	58.3
Rear track, ins.	58.1	59.0	59.0
Overall length, ins.	186.81	182.1	182.1
Width, ins.	70.9	69.2	69.2
Height, ins.	51.8	47.8	47.8
Front suspension	Independent with coil spring	Independent with coil spring	Independent with coil spring
Rear suspension	Hotchkiss type w/semi-elliptic multi-leaf	Independent with fixed differential and multi-leaf transverse spring	

Otherwise, headroom is not a problem. Nor is legroom a limiting factor. We did find that a six-footer, or thereabouts, develops a tired leg on all but full throttle runs. Moderate gas pedal application causes the driver's knee to bend without having adequate thigh support. A large, softly upholstered roll, à la hot-rodder's technique on channeled cars, would do away with the annoying nonsupport.

The semireclining seatbacks are enjoyable. We found ourselves hunching forward at first, but then learned to settle back, giving us plenty of comfort and also a just-right distance to the wheel.

Ride qualities of all but the biggest-engined car are surprising. Bounce and rebound are relatively calm, especially for a sports car. The inside quietness is something we never expected in a two-placer, though a good many imported sporty cars have this. The flow-through ventilation works, making for windows-up driving in all but the hottest weather.

Difficulty in entry and exit—for the average person—is just something sports car owners should expect. Considering this car is short of four feet in height, we'd have to rate it good.

COBRA

Handling
Better than most domestic cars—firm with plenty of control—just slightly below that of all-out sports car.

Ride
Stiff but not abusive.

Comfort
Not bad, but seats could stand refinement. Rear seat room is very marginal.

Quality
Surprising. Vast improvement over '67s.

Performance
Adequate for car's intended use.

We like
Most of the styling—ease of operation—shoulder harnesses and roll bar.

We don't like
Phony "mag" hubcaps that ruin looks, too light trunk lid and too-open hood louvers, obstructed forward vision, lack of greater distinction from Mustang.

CORVETTE

Handling
Best of all U.S. cars, and one of the upper echelon of sports "handlers."

Ride
Good on all but the big-engined, 435-horsepower cars are abusive to passengers.

Comfort
Very good on long trips as well as in-town, interior access is difficult for all but the very agile.

Quality
Needs upgrading, but is progressively getting better.

Performance
Good, and better than its competitor. Has the best potential.

We like
Style, instrumentation, lamp monitors, four-wheel disc brakes, good tractability.

We don't like
Leaky bodies, front ends that end past line of vision, unreachable left seatback release, absence of control lighting and good interior illumination.

OPTIONS & PRICES

	428 Cobra	427 Corvette
Mfg.'s suggested price	$4,317.39 Coupe	$4,636.00 Coupe
	$4,438.91 Convertible	$4,320.00 Convertible
Engine options		105.35 350 hp
		200.15 390 hp
		305.50 400 hp
		437.00 435 hp
4-speed transmission	Standard	184.35
Auto transmission	50.08	237.00
Limited-slip differential		46.35
Hi-perf. tires	Standard	31.30
Special suspension	Standard	36.90
HD ignition	N/A	73.75
Adj. steer. column	66.14	42.15
Power steering	84.47	94.80
Power disc brakes	64.77	42.15
Power windows	N/A	57.95
Air conditioning	356.10	412.90
AM radio	57.59	N/A
AM/FM radio	181.36 (Stereo)	172.75
Fold-down rear seat	64.78	N/A

Plus & Minus Features

"Rain, Rain, go away." We sang that song for a solid week. The Corvette handles admirably in the wet, but passengers didn't fare too well in our test convertible. The 350-horsepower car came with the removable hardtop, and oddly enough it leaked, and the soft top didn't. We found the major source of water-fill at the rear corners of the side windows, but weren't able to fix it on our own. A couple of comments on this have drifted in from '68 owners, and though they've cured the ill, it was a nuisance.

The hidden wipers should help prolong blade life, and they undoubtedly benefit appearance. We had a difficult time explaining this to the gas station attendant who gashed his finger on the nonflush fitting door edge corner. Seems something was keeping the cover from going flush to the cowl, and he found out about it the hard way.

The glove compartment is behind the seat, along with the other identical-looking hatches. One holds the jack, and the other—right behind the driver—contains the battery. Be careful which one you reach for.

Regardless of its few distinct minus points, the Corvette still holds the position of one of the world's all-out "class" vehicles, and justifiably so. Kinda wish we had one.

JAGUAR XKE V-12 vs. CORVETTE LT-1 V-8

ERIC DAHLQUIST
Motor Trend, April 1971

After 10 years Jaguar finally puts its super V-12 into the XKE.
And you know what, the small-block Chevy is still better.

THE XKE. How we all yearned after it in 1963. That and Sting Rays. A guy named Tony Schuler put the deal dead into perspective: "If you're gonna buy anything, it'll be a Sting Ray because you get parts for it and they don't rust. But in three years a Sting Ray will look old and Jaguar will probably have a waiting list for the last XKE they build." In the frigid reality of a Buffalo winter, we all knew Schuler had the word.

Besides that, there was one insurmountable handicap with the XKE. Beneath those undulating curves of satin metal skin, flowing over the chassis like windblown filaments of smoke, was a six—an inline six-cylinder engine. Yes, it had a brace of overhead cams sheathed by the most official-looking valve covers known to man, and a rappy sound from the twinned exhaust pipes shot out from under the center of the car. But after all, it was really only an upbeat variation of the same engine the XK-120 had had in 1949, and even the original Jaguar SS in 1936, and it was a slug by '63 standards. Everyone knew there was a V-8 or V-12 coming because it had been coming since about 10 years ago. When it happened, the XKE performance situation would be set right once and for all—the fuel-injected 327 plastic cars—heavens, not even cars, things, would be humbled.

Schuler was wrong and right at the same time. Sting Rays became familiar but somehow never contemptible—even through the mako shark evolution and power fertilizations like the aluminum-block ZL1. Jaguar, in the interim, re-issued the same old power plant, albeit bored out from 3.8 to 4.2 liters, and kept selling each yearly XKE quota not because they were superior to other cars that came along, but because the machine apparently represents what America's genteel automobile society apparently wants in their sports cars—a sort of Wedgewood china finish, the accurate look (but ill-function) of Smith's gauges, the smell of real leather upholstery, wood-rimmed steering wheels that crack with time if not cared for, and expensive, fitful maintenance that is a status symbol itself. Jaguar achieved immortality by creating models that looked like they cost twice as much as they did. An XKE fit into the passing scene in West Palm Beach in the '60s like Stutzes had in the '20s;

The Jaguar's undulating curves of metal skin contrast with the Corvette's brutish flares and bulges.

the only thing it lacked was a Fitzgerald to write about it. The trouble with Corvettes from the beginning was that anyone could own one. And because of it the car inevitably equated with eight-inch slicks, custom mags, and the other badges of America's affluent young. Not to forget that Corvettes change hands like money. It is some kind of ultimate, inverse status symbol that the life expectancy of a new 'Vette in New York City is one hour, before it is stolen and stripped.

About a year ago now, rumors of a Jaguar V-something began to be more than speculation. Jaguar's brilliant engine designer, George Mundy, was finally surfacing with one of the many configurations he had worked up over the years since Jaguar won Le Mans in 1955–56 with the fantastic D-types, machines that went like the hammers and cost as much as they looked they cost. Jaguar has lived on the reputation ever since. Of course, the actual item, a real V-8 or V-12 Jaguar XKE could not be expected to just be engineered up, tested, and announced. Their fantastically successful XJ-6 sedan, pretender to Mercedes carriage trade title in the luxuriant southern California market, burst upon an unsuspecting world with such triumph that the factory probably figured it should try it again. Word that the all-new job was to be formally debuted at the New York Auto Show was very quietly leaked to selected members of the automotive press corps and the pecking order of publications to be privileged by a preannouncement road test struck into bronze.

But not without some preconditions. Jaguar and its West Coast distributor, Charles H. Hornburg, requested assurance that should we be given a car for just two days and that we would not conduct a full-on evaluation because the machines available were engineering prototypes and not truly representative. The rules of the house were driving impressions only. And, actually, what more would a buyer do? Except, maybe try a Jaguar and then a

The LT-1 has angles and flares going off in all directions while the E-type is rounded and smooth. Not an actual 2+2, the Jag has larger interior.

'Vette and buy the one he liked best, right? Well, that's the approach we took. Chevrolet, for its part supplied a very normal 3,583-pound four-speed, which, with 330-horsepower 350-cid V-8, compared very favorably with the 2,800-pound 326-cid V-12. Chevy was as interested as any of us to know how the engines stacked up because some of the V-12's significant specifications (like power and torque) were very close.

Mr. C. H. Hornburg personally greeted us at his Sunset Boulevard outlet and led us around back to meet a surprise—a vehicle that looked virtually unchanged from any contemporary 2+2 coupe except for the new grille opening and unobtrusive fender flares above the tires. XKE styling, which had been the best there was 10 years ago, and which has slid backward with every slight restyle since, hit a new nadir. Even if the V-12 is a smasher, style-conscious Jaguar, who has been up to the task of living with a six with swoopy lines all these years, must realize it needs a new car as well.

As Hornburg lifted up the hood/fender assembly that pivots forward ahead of the aluminum-cone radiator, there was the engine that, at first apprehension, seemed hardly larger than the old sixes he had out front in the showroom guarded by a wizened English salesman. But it was. The frame stubs for the engine were 26.5 inches wide, 9.5 inches farther apart than the six. To the untrained eye, it looked as though Jaguar had summarily swapped in a 12 for a 6 and let it go at that, but with all the minor changes in track (up 4½ inches front, 3½ inches rear), the new engine bay, 109-inch wheelbase (four inches greater than before) with the same 184.5-inch overall length and strengthened driveline, it was evident a lot of reengineering was required. Perhaps a small-block Chevy would have been easier. But then, you couldn't have that Lincoln-Zephyr–looking distributor cap. Of course, Mr. Hornburg didn't know any of this then; he probably still doesn't. In fact, neither did anyone else in North America.

Corvettes, now, that's a different story. Veritable reams of facts and figures have emanated throughout the land until almost any nine-year-old can tell you the LT-1 is really a detoxed Z-28 with 48 more cubic inches. On balance, the Corvette is 7.5 inches shorter than the XKE (182.5 to 190 inches), 3.75 inches wider (69 to 65.25), 2.2 inches lower (47.8 to 50), and most significantly, possesses a 4.2-inch greater front track (58.7 to 54.5 inches) and a 5.9-inch bigger rear (59.4 to 53.5-inch).

As for suspension, both vehicles can be said to be fully independent, except the Jag has torsion bars in front where the Corvette uses coils and four shock/coils in back, contrasted with a multi-leaf transverse spring. The main difference between the two was that the LT-1 had a close-ratio four-speed and the XKE a three-speed automatic.

Getting in for the first time we were surprised that the 50-inch-high 2+2 coupe, though two inches taller than the Corvette, is much more difficult to enter because of the high, wide door sills and rather narrow doors. There, bedded in a leather-covered dash were all the instruments you would ever need, speedo, tach, ammeter, oil pressure, clock, temperature, and fuel—Smiths every one, lettered with the precision of a Rolex watch. When you put the turn signal on over about 2,000 rpm, the tach needle jumped with every pulse of the flasher, but who cares?

With the cockpit check run-through, the first-time driver is surprised at the narrow interior, the out-of-proportion length-to-width ratio of the car, and the way the torpedo front fenders just shoot out into the distance.

The only thing wrong with the Jaguar V-12 engine is that the mufflers muffle too much. Writers will spend hours trying to get just how those six pairs of 9.0:1 compression pistons articulate on the listening air, but it is so deliciously unique, they will fail. You blip the throttle and there is this neat subdued brrrrrapp! brrrrrap!—a kind of satin-finished Ferrari echo. The price of XKE V-12 admission will unquestionably be at least two grand more than the DOHC six, but it will all be worth it every time you blip the throttle or run the gears.

And that is another thing, running through the gears feels pretty good. Showing no apparent strain, the XKE clicked off 14.83 seconds, 96.72 miles per hour in the quarter-mile and 7.2 seconds 0–60, handicapped as it was with what felt like about a 2.23 final drive ratio. Significantly, while most engines find one happy place or other on the rev band where they really come-on-the cam, so to speak, the Jaguar feels equally strong through its entire range and is very quiet about it as well.

Of course the LT-1 was faster. Even with an untuned engine the thing zipped a 14.30-second quarter at 98 miles per hour. Given a four-speed the XKE could be very close, closer than you would imagine because the V-12 is so smooth. And, while we were there, we also made a few orbits of the OCIR skid pad. Looping around the 100-foot circle the Corvette generated .06 g more lateral acceleration (.823 to .761), but that was only the half of it. The XKE tended to understeer when pushed (as the 'Vette oversteered or was neutral), as well as overheat, or at least show higher on the temperature gauge than it did in rush hour traffic, which was plenty high. Running hot has been Jaguar's Achilles' heel for as long as the automaker has been bringing the things

The XKE instrument panel is well designed with precise-looking dials, rocker switches.

The XKE's engine compartment looks crammed and it is. Still, the lift away front fender assembly makes vital parts accessible. The engine is a hot runner.

over here, and in these days of the obvious advantages of sealed cooling systems, there is no excuse for it. Air conditioning is almost standard equipment on XKEs and you suspect the car's tendency to overheat would put the refrigeration unit out of play at the very time you needed it.

At the end of our compressed two-day impression period we could say this about the XKE V-12 and Corvette: Far and away the Jaguar is better finished and sounder constructed because it has, after all, an all-steel unit body on which is lavished a lot of particular attention. Inside, the English have demonstrated a visible superiority in stitching up a fine set of hides and there are no loose ends or threads hanging. Compared with the Corvette's street-racer exhaust, the XKE is a soundproofed transportation capsule, an effect that is completely ruined by a loud rear end whine at 67–72 miles per hour—precisely where you would normally cruise. Still, the low noise level is superb at all other speeds and probably one reason why the car has sustained its demand. The Jaguar's automatic transmission is relatively

JAGUAR XKE V-12 vs. CORVETTE LT-1 V-8

ENGINES	Jaguar XKE V-12	Corvette LT-1
No. of cylinders:	12	8
Layout:	Vee, 60 degrees	Vee, 90 degrees
Bore:	3.54-inch (90 mm)	4.00-in.
Stroke:	2.76-inch (70 mm)	3.48-in.
Displacement:	326 ci	350 ci
Horsepower:	314 @ 6,200	330 @ 5,600 rpm
Torque:	349 ft-lb @ 3,800	360 ft-lb @ 4,000
Compression ratio:	9.0:1	9.0:1
Ignition:	Lucas capacitor discharge	Delco capacitor discharge
Carburetion:	Four, 1.75-in. bore	One, 1.686-in. bore
	Zenith-Strombergs	Holley 4 barrel
Total weight:	680 lbs.	550 lbs.
CHASSIS		
Overall length:	190 in.	182.5 in.
Overall height:	50 in.	47.8 in.
Overall width:	65.25 in.	69 in.
Track – front:	54.5 in.	58.7 in.
rear:	53.5 in.	59.4 in.
Weight:	2,800 lbs.	3,593 lbs.
Fuel Consumption:	11.1–14 gal.	8.1–14 gal.

7.2   10.3   3.1

Jaguar

5.9   9.3   3.0

Corvette

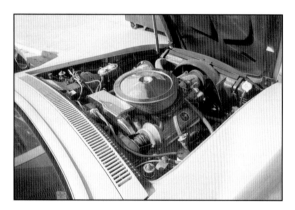

The LT-1 350 is not exactly the mechanic's dream of serviceability, but at least parts are available at the local Chevrolet parts department.

smooth shifting and the V-12 will get you away from all but determined stoplight protagonists. Surely, air conditioning will not bog it if you can keep the engine cool.

And that should be about the old ball game … except for one thing—the Corvette is a better car. Even with its periodic unbeautification program, the XKE still has more integral styling than Corvette, which, with its flares and bulges has the same sort of blunt, brute statement as Jimmy Doolittle's Gee Bee of prewar Cleveland air race fame. But, that's what most Americans understand. They will also understand that the XKE V-12 just doesn't feel as at home on the road as the Sting Ray, does not possess anywhere near the handling nor road feel in the steering. True, the Corvette's fiberglass body does creak a bit but it is not loose by any means and even if it rides harsher, the paint doesn't fade in the Texas sun, and the body won't rust, even in Buffalo. For all the XKE's luxurious interior the function and reach of the driver's tools are no better than the 'Vette. Chevrolet's seats hold you much better and the inertia-reel three-point safety harness arrangement may be the best in any car.

As a cargo ship the Jag is vastly more desirable than the 'Vette because of its 2+2 configuration and hatchback trunk lid. Still, some of the car's utility is tempered by the fact the car is really a two-passenger model with a jump seat and is not primarily intended to carry 4-foot-by-8-foot sheets of plywood anyway.

If and when Jaguar sees fit to mate an entirely modern design with what seems on the surface a very competent engine, the effect might be truly remarkable. The XJ-6 was, but then, how many XJ-6s come along in your lifetime?

At the end of this, we were almost embarrassed to find that despite Detroit's myopia and failures it can still build one of the best cars anywhere, not for 9 or 10 grand, but 6. That's really what we're all about as a country.

ROAD TEST: CHEVROLET CORVETTE

ERIC DAHLQUIST
Motor Trend, January 1973

The Corvette isn't just America's only sports car.
It's America's last zoomy car.

THE FACT OF THE MATTER is that the Corvette is still the zoomiest car in America. You know it when you're on the way to Detroit's Metro Airport and you pass a Ford Squire full of kids and they press to the side windows to get a better look at this Silver Metallic mako shark, train-lengthing the old man's Bekins moving van of a station wagon. Just the way Speed Racer would do it—fading off ahead, obviously over the speed limit. It's the Marty Milner/George Maharis Route 66 show all over again.

You know it again on the Ventura Freeway when some kid in a red Mazda mini-truck almost spins the head off his shoulders as he says to the girl next to him—you can read his lips—"That's the new 'Vette!"

Sure, you see a Pantera occasionally and maybe one Ferrari or a Lamborghini a year, but those are the cars of the chosen few, and this is America, where if we're privileged, we're not supposed to flaunt it, much less covet it.

If there has ever been a point to the Corvette since the original Blue Flame Six engine was replaced by something with hair on its chest, it is simply that, by and large, no other sports car has been as good or looked as wild for less than twice the price.

The Corvette is so typically American. Superficially, it is as exotic as a Swiss mermaid: acceleration only a dragster can match, independent suspension and disc brakes for all four wheels (features no other American car has), a Porsche Targalike lift-off roof, a futuristic fiberglass body, and enough gauges in the cockpit to keep track of a small war. But underneath beats the reliable heart of an Impala. And affordable. Anyone who well and truly wants to own a Corvette can (and usually does); GMAC will see to that. A very successful formula, thank you.

Well, if you believe everything you read in the funny papers, Detroit—not to mention America—has turned its back on "zoomy" cars, hot cars are dead, etc., etc. If true, the Corvette would likely be one of the first casualties. If safety regulations and public anti-speed sentiment couldn't kill it, surely escalating insurance rates would.

Grill-less side vents, a new nose, and a hood bulge account for major changes in the 1973 Corvette. New alloy wheels reduce unsprung weight by 40 pounds.

But of course you already know the 'Vette is alive and well, and that for 1973 it not only meets the new five-mile-per-hour no-damage (to "safety related items") bumpers but looks cleaner in the bargain.

Thanks to the "Omar" bolt.

Putting a '73 'Vette up on a hoist, Zora Arkus-Duntov, the Chevrolet engineer legendary as "the father of the Corvette," showed me an inconspicuous 3/8-inch bolt connecting the urethane-plastic-covered front bumper (body-paint covered) to the slightly beefed-up frame. Upon impact, this bolt extrudes itself through a 5/16-inch die, dissipating most of the energy of the collision in the process. Simple, cheap, and light—about 35 pounds.

Duntov, a White Russian by birth, a sometime race driver by avocation, and one of the few real "personalities" at General Motors (which frowns on anything but the low corporate profile), was obviously pleased with himself.

With a barely perceptible hiss, the hydraulic hoist deposited the '73 test car—a silver 'Vette powered by the big, 454-ci V-8 (option LS-4)—back on the ground, and Duntov and I set off for a trial spin around GM's proving grounds in Milford, Michigan.

The first thing I noticed was the fact that the new car was light-years ahead of the 'Vettes we tested last June in terms of road noise (or its absence) and ride comfort. Duntov said that the substitution of GR-15 radial-ply tires for last year's bias-belted tires were responsible. Additionally, although the new tires somewhat diminished the car's sheer cornering power on dry pavement, wet-driving characteristics were improved by the new radials.

The new tires required some slight recalibration of the suspension, as well as the addition of two-piece rubber-biscuit body mounts. Inside the body, asphalt sound deadener has been applied to almost all parts, along with generous stuffings of fiberglass insulation under foot as well as hood. Still, Duntov was not totally enthralled with the initial '73 production run because the assembly-line workers had not properly installed all of the sound package, and our test car was not as quiet as it was supposed to be. But a lot of the old fiberglass body squeaks and groans had been filtered out of the cockpit, along with some of the bone-rattling ride on rough surfaces. Surprisingly, the car still has its traditionally good road feel.

The car had optional leather interior with the luxuriant look and smell it should have, but somehow the legroom, which has never been extravagant in Corvettes, feels even more limited. In the translation from vinyl to leather, Duntov said, the seat designers have lost more than an inch of legroom. But Duntov couldn't figure out where, or even why the space was lost. So, if you're more than 6-foot-1, be advised to opt for standard upholstery.

Virtually unchanged since 1968, the '73 Corvette is revamped substantially to meet federal safety requirements; it comes off cleaner than the original version in the process.

The LS-4 is rated at 280 horsepower at 4,400 rpm, while torque is 395-ft-lb at 3,200 rpm. Simply stated, the 454 Corvette is now quicker through the gears overall and noticeably improved at the low end, a sensation quickly underscored during acceleration runs. For example, where our 1972 LS-5 did 0–30 in 3.1 seconds, the '73 LS-4 hit 30 in 2.7 seconds. Zero to 75 miles per hour was 10.1 seconds in last year's LS-5 and 9.7 in this year's LS-4.

The reason for this performance surge is a minor camshaft timing and lift revision and the new cowl-induction hood that is standard on all models. Cold outside air enters at the high-pressure area at the base of the windshield and is routed to the carburetor via an underhood duct. In the duct, an electrically operated solenoid modulates air flow according to throttle opening. The horsepower benefits of cold-air induction have been loudly trumpeted since the Pontiac Ram-Air GTO. But the high temperatures under the 'Vette's hood—a result of meeting new exhaust emissions requirements—was as much a factor in Chevrolet's decision to adopt the new induction arrangement. This is one of those twilight areas where what's good for emissions is also good for performance.

When Duntov and company adjourned to the skid pad, the effect of the radial tires was clearly evident. In 1972, the bias-belted tires (F70-15 Polyglass) generated a maximum cornering force of .83 g. But now, a model-year later, the LS-4 is a .75-g car.

Straight-line stopping was not a replay of the skid pad. In fact, the radial tire LS-4 stopped 2 feet shorter from 30 miles per hour than the LS-5's 29 feet. Sixty to 0 was another matter. Here it was a job to get the LS-4 hauled down in 135 feet, while last year a 122-foot average was easy with the LS-5.

We didn't have the opportunity to try out the '73 car on wet roads, but it isn't for nothing that at least one manufacturer of radial-ply tires calls its product "The Rain Tire." Radials are notably less skittish on slippery roads, and their adoption on the Corvette should go a long way towards providing a truly versatile road car in the European sense.

Phase two of this test commenced when we took a 350-ci, L-82 option Corvette out to Orange County Raceway. The L-82 is an emissions-inspired hydraulic-cam version of last year's fire-breathing LT-1. There are two ramifications resulting from the lifters. First, horsepower in the 1973 car has dropped from 255 at 5,600 rpm to 250 at 4,000, but has gained five additional foot-pounds of torque over last year. Therefore, the engine has more midrange guts, is quieter, and certainly less a service problem.

Zora Arkus-Duntov (in sunglasses) explains the intricacies of a revitalized LS-4 engine for 1973. Cold-air, cowl-induction for the carburetor has improved performance and lowered emissions at the same time.

Last year's LT-1 with the close-ratio, four-speed transmission and 3.70:1 axle ratio could hit 60 miles per hour in 6.9 seconds. In 1973, despite the new, heavier front end for the five-mile-per-hour bumper, sound deadening package, air conditioning, a wide-ratio transmission, 3.55:1 final drive, and five less horsepower, the 0-60-mile-per-hour time for the new L-82 was still 7.3 seconds! More available torque at a lower specific rpm peak has helped, of course, but remember that Chevrolet has made a conspicuous effort to pare down weight (as well as cost). The Corvette's removable rear window is gone, as well as the hidden windshield-wiper panel and complicated fender air ducts. Another 40 pounds of unsprung weight was knocked off with optional slot-type aluminum wheels. In all, comparably equipped '73 models run about 30 pounds heavier than their 1972 counterparts.

The new L-82 Corvette may be one of the best things to happen to the American driver this year. The car is very quiet for a spirited sports machine, rides well, is more than quick enough to acquit itself well in stoplight Grand Prix, yet it has lost little of its nimbleness. Equipped with air conditioning (and a new coolant-recovery system that will never boil over—Chevrolet claims), the L-82 is the best Corvette Chevrolet has built in a long while.

That is not to say the L-82 or LS-4 were completely without fault. Drivability, no doubt due to emissions standards, was impaired by stalling during warmup and a slight hesitation when the throttle was quickly opened. The L-82 four-speed transmission was hard to get into low gear and the gate between first and third was far too narrow. As mentioned earlier, the legroom is cramped . . . especially for a two-seater car more than 15 feet long.

On balance, the '73 Corvettes—with either the small (350 V-8) or the large (454 V-8)—are several steps ahead of last year's models. They have lost little in the way of true performance and promise to gain substantially in something as important as driving in the rain.

There is a new Corvette in the wings for 1975, but even if it came in a year early, we wouldn't expect a single unsold '73. It's that good a car.

Driving the '73 Corvette is a better deal than ever before because the car has lost little all-round performance in the process of gaining immeasurably improved ride and lowered sound levels.

'73 vs. '72 CHEVROLET CORVETTE

SPECIFICATIONS	1972 454 COUPE	1973 454 COUPE	1972 LT-1	1973 L-82
Engine	90° V-8 OHV	90° V-8 OHV	90° V-8 OHV	90° V-8 OHV
Bore x stroke-in.	4.25 x 4.0	4.25 x 4.0	4.0 x 3.48	4.0 x 3.48
Displacement-ci	454	454	350	350
Hp @ rpm	270 @ 4,000	275 @ 4,400	255 @ 5,600	250 @ 5,200
Torque: ft-lb @ rpm	390 @ 3,200	395 @ 2,800	280 @ 4,000	285 @ 4,000
Compression ratio	8.25:1	8.5:1	9.0:1	9.0:1
Carburetion	1 4-barrel	1 4-barrel	1 4-barrel	1 4-barrel
Transmission	Turbo Hydra-Matic	Turbo Hydra-Matic	4-speed close ratio	4-speed
Final drive ratio	3.08:1	3.08:1	3.70:1	3.70:1
Steering type	Recirculating ball	Recirculating ball	Recirculating ball	Recirculating ball
Steering ratio	17.6:1	17.6:1	17.6:1	17.6:1
Turning diameter (curb-to-curb-ft.)	37.0	37.0	37.0	37.0
Wheel turns (lock-to-lock)	2.92	2.92	2.92	2.92
Tire size	F70 x 15	GR70 x 15	F70 x 15	GR70 x 15
Brakes	Disc/disc	Disc/disc	Disc/disc	Disc/disc
Front suspension	Single lower A arm, coil springs, concentric shocks	Single lower A arm, coil springs, concentric shocks	Single lower A arm, coil springs, concentric shocks	Single lower A arm, coil springs, concentric shocks
Rear suspension	Independent, fixed differential, transverse multi-leaf spring, lateral struts, shocks	Independent, fixed differential, transverse multi-leaf spring, lateral struts, shocks	Independent, fixed differential, transverse multi-leaf spring, lateral struts, shocks	Independent, fixed differential, transverse multi-leaf spring, lateral struts, shocks
Body/Frame Construction	Unitized	Unitized	Unitized	Unitized
Wheelbase, in.	98.0	98.0	98.0	98.0
Overall Length, in.	182.5	184.7	182.5	184.7
Width, in.	69.0	69.0	69.0	69.0
Height, in.	47.8	47.8	47.8	47.8
Front track, in.	58.7	58.7	58.7	58.7
Rear track, in.	59.4	59.5	59.4	59.5
Curb weight, lbs.	3,725	3,725	3,356	3,356
Fuel capacity, gal.	18	18	18	18
Oil capacity, qt.	6	6	5	5

PERFORMANCE	454 COUPE	454 COUPE	LT-1	L-82
Acceleration				
0–30 mph	3.8	2.7	2.9	2.9
0–45 mph	4.9	4.6	4.8	4.8
0–60 mph	6.8	6.8	6.9	7.3
0–75 mph	10.1	9.7	10.2	10.2
Standing start quarter-mile				
Mph	93	93	92	92
Elapsed time	14.1	14.1	14.3	14.3
Passing speeds				
40–60 mph	2.8	2.8	2.8	2.8
50–70 mph	3.3	3.3	3.6	3.6
Mph per 1,000 rpm				
(in top gear)	25.0	25.0	23.5	23.5
Stopping distances				
From 30 mph	29.1 ft.	26.3 ft.	17.9 ft.	25.2 ft.
From 60 mph	122.9	135.3	116.0	122.9
Gas mileage range	13–15 mpg	13–15 mpg	9–12 mpg	9–12 mpg
MT road test score	78.8	79.1	82.3	84.3

ROAD TEST COMPARISON: CORVETTE AND BRICKLIN

JIM BROKAW
Motor Trend, May 1975

THE 'GLASS WAR

SINCE THE BEGINNING in 1953 when the Corvette had a six-cylinder engine, a two-speed slush box transmission, and came only in white, challengers have been many, but conquerors none. The two-seater T-Bird gave up and went fancy, the iron riding British sports cars never had a chance, even the vaunted Shelby Cobra lacked the staying power to maintain the challenge. Just as it seemed there would be an end to this meddling combat, along comes the Bricklin.

You mention Bricklin and Corvette in the same breath and you get an instant denial from both camps. Tony Kopp, West Coast frontman for the Bricklin Vehicle Corporation, instantly poo-poos the suggestion that they would dare take cudgel against the undisputed champion. However, there's only one other two-seater, plastic-bodied sporty car in town. The Chevrolet folks dismiss the Bricklin as a feeble effort with little to redeem itself save the flying doors. It is still the only other plastic-bodied two-seater in town.

Is there a valid challenge from the little pointy-nosed upstart? There is indeed. A clear and present challenge from the standpoint of the Bricklin's uniqueness, and a very real future challenge if the Bricklin people can get their act together.

Dimensionally they are remarkably similar. The Bricklin's wheelbase is 96 inches, the Corvette's, 98 inches. Overall length is 178.6 inches for Bricklin, 185.2 inches for Corvette. Bricklin is 67.6 inches wide and 48.25 inches high; Corvette measures 69.0 inches across and 48.1 inches tall. Corvette weighs in at 3,660 lbs. with Bricklin tipping a mere 3,530 lbs.

Partially from smog regulations, partially from elevated cost of production, and partially from frightening insurance rates, the present model of the Corvette is very nearly domesticated. Our particular test car had the California L-48 engine, a 350-4V of limited spirit. The L-82 is more sprightly, but not for us on the West Coast.

Driving the 'Vette gives one a distinct feeling of being in a tunnel. The deeply recessed primary instrument pods, the layback seats, the clearly visible, long hood, and the sharply raked windshield all combine to visually place the car out in front of you. The large-diameter

A Bricklin SV-1 and Chevrolet Corvette Stingray go head to head in road testing.

skinny rim steering wheel seems a bit out of place, but that may be because of driver prejudice in favor of small-diameter fat steering wheels.

Corvette's dash and instrument layout is very good, but it still takes a bit of neck craning to read them all. The console is very well laid out with neat control wheels for the "environment control" system; however, one has to lean forward to tune the radio.

Leatherlike seat upholstery looks great but isn't the toughest in town. Air vents are well located and function nicely, particularly the "B" pillar blower vent.

Corvette has a few subtle niceties such as the peanut light behind the rearview mirror, but surprisingly lacks a few expected refinements. The flap-pocket glove compartment just doesn't make it. Lack of space between seat side and door panel makes the acquisition of seatbelts a chore. The hardtop convertible panels are easily removed, but insertion into the rear storage cave is cumbersome and very conducive to damaging seat back upholstery and chipping interior paint. The headlight manual erect switch and the "B" pillar blower switch are unlabeled, which is not a problem once you learn their location but certainly an oversight.

Interior fit and finish of seams and panels is not what we have learned to expect from GM. Windshield top chrome molding is very poorly bonded on. Exterior panel fit is better but could stand improvement. Exterior finish however is very good. Flush fitting scoop-latch door handles are a class touch. The power windows work superbly and greatest of all are the magnificent sounds growling from under the hood when you stand on the gas pedal.

Under the hood 'Vette has well-shielded electrical wiring, metal-protected, silicone-covered spark plug wires, a viscous-clutch fan, and easily reached accessory drive units. The spark plugs themselves are not so easily reached.

The high-energy ignition system is virtually moisture proof and breakerless to increase planned spark plug life from 6,000 miles to 20,000 miles. Corvette's exclusive exhaust system gives the 350 a slight horsepower edge over the standard version of the engine; however full potential was never realized when the twin 160-cid catalytic converters had to be scrapped in favor of a single 260-cid converter when the smaller devices failed durability tests.

On the road, Corvette is a firm riding nicely handling fun car to drive. With that long hood and the cropped-up fenders looming into full view, all that is required is to point the

On the road, the Corvette (in the rear) is a firm riding nicely handling fun car to drive. With that long hood and the cropped-up fenders looming into full view, all that is required is to point the beast and it very properly goes where it's told.

beast and it very properly goes where it's told. The coil front springs with a new front stabilizer bar of 0.875-inch diameter works very nicely with the 10 leaf transverse rear spring, increased from the 9-leaf spring of '74.

In fact the Corvette is disarmingly well behaved throughout most of its operating envelope. On the track the hidden beast bares its fangs. When you're getting it on, the 'Vette still goes where it is pointed, but you'd best point with a light hand and a bit of skill. Braking lightly into a corner brings the tail around just right for storming out under full throttle, with that magnificent howling of the cold-air induction bellowing like it had power, exiting as neat as you please. Through the zig-zag chicame portion of our handling course, all is well until you reach the limit.

Without so much as a snarl it reaches back and bites you when you push too hard. When she lets go, the rear end sneaks around quietly until it's too late to do anything but hang on and steer backwards.

The secret pretender to the throne is not yet in the same ballpark with the Corvette, but the problems are all correctable. And therein lies the threat, if the Bricklin folks get it together, including getting their escalating costs under control, the 'Vette is going to get a run for the crown. Like the 'Vette, the Bricklin SV-1 (Safety Vehicle-1) is a plastic car. An acrylic outer shell over a fiberglass sandwich gives it a shiny gloss. Paint is impregnated and should not fade but that is something one believes upon sight of proof.

We tested both the American Motors–engined '74 model and the Ford-motored '75 version. We found the '74 model, AMC 360-4V engine to be better performing and easier to control than the '75 with a Ford 351-2V engine. The '74 felt more responsive on the street and more controllable on the track. Into a max performance turn, the '74 went from

Dimensionally the Corvette Stingray (left) and Bricklin SV-1 are remarkably similar. The Bricklin's wheelbase is 96 inches, the Corvette's, 98 inches. Overall length is 178.6 inches for Bricklin, 185.2 inches for Corvette. Bricklin is 67.6 inches wide and 48.25 inches high.

understeer, to neutral to oversteer, controllable with power, in a very predictable fashion. Reaction was quick with lots of input to the driver.

The '74 model (both models utilize a Javelin suspension, with coil front springs and leaf rears with front stabilizer bar) had lost the light, quick reactive feeling. In order to accommodate the heavier Ford engine, mounting points had to be moved and spring rates were changed. The spring guesser didn't do as well on the '75. A softer ride ensued at the sacrifice of handling and sensitivity. On the road the ride is smoother but also less stimulating, and you do buy a car like the Bricklin to be stimulated either by the car or its potential passengers. There is more body lean, though slight, and a sensation of tire roll-under. Likely the loss in handling is a combination of too slow a spring rate and too much lean, which does not keep a full tire footprint on the working pavement.

Those wonderful gullwing doors. The eight-second cycle time is not excessive, once you learn how to use them. In a heavy rain, they leak like a sieve. Bricklin has replacement boots, but we don't know if they are the kind that seal doors or the kind you wear.

Power was more brisk in the AMC version. Since the Ford trans reacted worse than any Ford trans we've driven (and we've flogged a number of FMX trans-equipped cars), we suspect a clapped-out box, but that's what we tested and that's what we have to judge. Both versions edged the Corvette on the drag strip, but the 'Vette was noticeably slower shifting than the Torqueflite-equipped '74. The difference between the Corvette and the Ford-engined Bricklin was miniscule.

Outside, the Bricklin looks pretty sharp with reasonably good matching of the few body seams exposed. Inside is a whole different ball game. This is where the homework is needed. There is no ashtray and no cigarette lighter. Mr. Bricklin announces in his brochure that smoking is dangerous and he will not have a hazard in his vehicle. Fine and noble. I smoke and I want a real ashtray, not a beanbag that I would have to purchase if I owned one. Nonsmokers rejoice. Mr. Bricklin failed to mention why he omitted any cockpit storage compartments.

Bricklin's rear deck area is well planned and neatly laid out. Storage is limited but accessible.

The driver environment is a contrast between excellent and poor. The seat is very well upholstered, well contoured, and firmly comfortable. It does not have an adjustable rake. I'm 5 foot, 10 inches tall and my head hits the roof. Dave Carlton who is 6 foot, 3 inches tall has to slouch to fit.

The armrests are too narrow and poorly located. There is no remote right-hand mirror control. With the limited visibility through the rear window, both outside mirrors are

Bricklin's good points and shortcomings are clearly visible. The poorly placed steering wheel obscures a well-designed instrument panel. The excellent quality upholstery is diminished by rough trim edges and carelessly anchored carpeting.

The Corvette's interior reflects the years of refinement. Easily removable roof panels offer convertible exposure with hardtop safety and comfort. How you sit is how you fit. The 'Vette with adjustable rake seatback provides ample room for a 5-foot, 8-inch tall passenger.

mandatory and must be properly adjusted. The radio is great with magnificent sounds, but no pushbuttons to lock-in your favorite station. The radio in the '75 model suffered an undetermined malfunction before we acquired the vehicle. Dash layout is excellent with a full set of instruments, but the engine gauges are unlabeled.

The '74 steering wheel (small diameter, adjustable) was well placed, but the '75 version was set too low, blocking most of the dash instruments. We were informed that our test car, one of the first off the '75 line, was the only one with this fault. We'll believe when we see.

The digital clock is a nice touch, easily read.

Although the quality of the interior vinyl is excellent, the trimming is poor. The handbrake boot has ragged edges, and the door piston boot is the same. The trim on the edge of the center console should be improved.

Paint on the inside top door sill is poorly applied. Carpeting is not properly anchored.

The rear deck area is well planned and quite functional, unless you order an optional spare tire. Then the rear deck will be crowded. The battery is located in the rear deck behind the passenger seat. It is hard to get at, particularly when the front seat backs do not fold forward. The rear deck carpeting is properly anchored and very well planned with minimum seam exposure.

The rear deck lid hydraulic struts work very well. Both the rear deck lid and the magnificent gullwing doors can be opened from either the inside or the outside. There is a key-actuated external hydraulic lock for the doors.

Those grand and glorious doors are really a kick for the first couple of days. Then you enter phase two, where the novelty has worn off. We were constantly trying to climb out through the closed doors.

Phase three is when you remember the time it takes to open and close the doors—eight seconds. It's more convenient to open the doors as you roll up to your destination, also very dramatic. They can be safely opened at low speed, but it is not recommended at cruising speed.

The Bricklin boasts of being primarily a safety car. The front bumper is claimed to withstand "in excess of" five miles per hour. We didn't test it, but we know it will take five miles per hour and should take close to 10 miles per hour. The difference is that Bricklin's bumpers were designed with the car and do not have that hung-on look. They stick out just as far as any of the ugly ones.

The internal frame functions as a roll cage. Judging from the thickness of the windshield "A" pillar, which blocks vision noticeably, it should do the trick.

The lower perimeter frame runs very high around the passenger compartment and should perform the design function of occupant protection for moderate side intrusion impacts.

While the Bricklin doesn't really come on strong at the track, it is great fun to drive on the street. Handling is firm but not harsh. The steering lacks feel but is quick enough for exciting turns. Response is enough for the street but not crisp. The big plus is aerodynamics. There is minimal wind resistance. It feels like it could glide forever on a run down at the strip.

Fuel economy was refreshingly good, 17.8 miles per gallon on the '74 and 20.27 on the '75. Both were run on our 73-mile fuel test loop with a mixture of driving and traffic conditions. We ran the 'Vette over the same loop logging 16.5 miles per gallon.

The Bricklin is essentially an excellent concept with a firm beginning. The fit, finish, and trim problems can all be ironed out. The reduction in handling in the '75 can be corrected. Adjustable seat backs are not hard to find, and the fact that there is no passenger compartment storage can be rectified. The question is will it be done, and when will it be done?

The price has inflated from $7,490 for the '74 to $9,775 for the '75, compared to $8,227 for the Corvette (as tested in all cases). The 'Vette is much more refined and civilized, but the doors don't go up and down.

Corvette still owns the field, but the challenge is there and the Bricklin can be made into a very nice little hustler.

A BRICKLIN OWNER SPEAKS OUT

We've been attempting to locate a Bricklin owner for some months now, and shortly before we acquired our own test vehicle, Mitchell Schwartz of Sherman Oaks, California, telephoned us up—he owned a Bricklin.

He bought his 1974 Bricklin in late December for $7,685, and has spent considerable time examining the machine to "see how it was all put together." After racking up 7,300 miles on his car, Schwartz knows the Bricklin very well indeed.

What does it mean to be a Bricklin owner? Well, first of all it means 22 people a day asking, "What is it?" And, after telling them, it means 19 of them saying, "What in the hell is that?" Secondly, it means having a car where the thoughts behind it were building a sleekly styled, sexy body around proven American parts. In most ways Bricklin has accomplished that, although at this particular time the assembly of these ideas could stand some improvement.

As a former driver and "repairer" of three Ferraris, three Lamborghinis, two Panteras, a Maserati, a Jensen, a BMW, an Iso Rivolta, a Corvette, a 240Z and a few other off-beat cars, I consider myself a good judge of sports cars. How does a Bricklin stand up against these cars? Well, it doesn't accelerate like a Ferrari, but you don't have to check the oil pressure every time you wind it out. It doesn't corner like a Lamborghini, but you don't have to remove suspension parts to replace the starter. It doesn't feel like a mid-engined race car like a Pantera, but you don't have to be a gymnast to change the spark plugs. It is not as quiet as a Jensen, but at least all of the fuses are in one place. It doesn't have the prestige of a Maserati, but it runs exceptionally well and gets respectable gas mileage. It has more interior room than a Corvette and looks more solid than a "Z." So, I guess what I am saying is that it isn't an exotic car that you constantly have to worry about. What it is, is a reliable, tremendously drivable sports car.

I have had some problems, but all are assembly problems, not design problems. It has leaked a considerable amount of water in a heavy rain, but this problem has been worked out by the factory in later models and can be fixed by the service centers on earlier cars. I took Malcolm Bricklin for a ride in my car. He expressed his desire for the owners to suggest improvements. He is sending his head engineer out to look at my car, as I have modified mine in many of the problem areas, and he feels the assembly could be improved with some of these modifications.

I drove across country immediately after buying the car and encountered no mechanical problems whatsoever. There were a few comfort problems, such as cold air leaking into the car because of poor weather seals on the doors. The heater controls were not adjusted correctly for air flow so it worked at about half capacity. The dashboard squeaks, but the factory is working on that problem. I don't get the hoped-for 20 miles per gallon, but I do get a respectable 15.3 in the city and 17.3 on the road.

One other aspect worth mentioning is the attitude of the people within the organization. Every single person I have talked to at the company has taken a sincere interest in satisfying me and rectifying any problem as quickly as possible—not as cheaply as possible. Any problem or request for information has been handled graciously and promptly. It is a pleasant surprise compared to "Hans is too busy to fool mit die Einspritzer."
—Mitchell Schwartz

ROAD TEST: CORVETTE '77

TONY SWAN
Motor Trend, December 1976

The name's the same, but the dream is changing.

FLASHBACK: It's 1958 and a young man whiles away the hours preceding the arrival of a fresh issue of *Hot Rod* with one of his favorite fantasies—a smiling Zora Arkus-Duntov, for reasons best known to himself, is handing over the keys to a brand-new Corvette loaded up with every go-fast device known to man.

Flash forward: It's 1976 and the fantasy has somehow become reality. There are changes from the original scenario, of course, as you'd expect after two decades. The guy pushing the keys toward me is named Dave McLellan, chief engineer for the Corvette since Duntov's retirement two years ago. And the machine that matches my keys is hardly the rip-snorting stoplight stormer of my triple-carbureted youth. The go has been legislated down to conform with the unleaded era and the packaging has undergone endless refinement. But electric windows and contour bucket seats never hurt anyone, and the brute horsepower that Duntov once envisioned for the Corvette hasn't much place in the 55-mile-per-hour world of the safety nazis. And as McLellan notes, "It's still the fastest car made in America."

Then McLellan, astonishingly boyish-looking for his 39 years, and his top lieutenant Jim "Jingles" Ingle begin embellishing my 20-year-old fantasy as we stroll through the engineering garages at the GM proving grounds near Milford, Michigan. The idea is that I'm to pick up one of the very first of the 1977 Corvettes and drive it back to California, where John Christy and Chuck Nerpel will perform their various *Motor Trend* instrumented rituals on it. But in the meantime McLellan and Jingles are making sure I'll have fun with it.

McLellan is giving me one of those invitations you can't believe you're hearing: "Don't be afraid to run it hard. One of the best engines we ever had came out of a press test car with 15,000 miles on it. When we got it back, that engine was so fast and so loose we just took it out and saved it."

Jingles, a bespectacled towhead with the look of a fanatic about him, is leafing through my road atlas and gesturing at some obscure roads in southern Indiana and northern Kentucky.

"We've been on these roads here," he says. "They're interesting, and you can do pretty much whatever you want."

"The problem with the roads in the western part of the country is that they're not as challenging," says McLellan. "Now here—(he points at some squiggly lines connecting tiny dots with improbable names like Napolean and Ballstown)— you've got some nice up and down stuff, where you can get airborne now and then, and some great decreasing-radius turns."

Swell. Gimme the keys, Dave.

My new car is Corvette Dark Red, one of nine new colors for '77; the only color continuing from 1976 is Classic White. Like most of the changes for the new Corvette, it's almost subliminal. About the only other visible differences in the basic 'Vette are a couple of minor trim touches. The word Stingray has disappeared from the sides above the front fenderwell air scoops, there are new crossed-flag emblems front

Perhaps the most highly visible change to the 1977 Corvette is one of the new options—tinted transparent removable T-top roof panels. Not only do they lend a more open feeling to the interior, they're very helpful if you're on the lookout for aircraft.

and rear, and the air inlet at the rear of the hood has disappeared. The Corvette design staff, under studio chief Jerry Palmer, has managed to lend a thinner look to the windshield pillars, which is consistent with the cleaner look overall.

Perhaps the most highly visible change to the car is one of the new options—tinted transparent removable T-top roof panels. Not only do they lend a more open feeling to the interior, they're very helpful if you're on the lookout for aircraft. To make the panels more useful, McLellan and friends have come up with an attachment for the luggage rack that allows the panels to be stored on the rear deck. It's functional and slick-looking besides. Slick is also an apt description for the new optional outside sport mirrors. They're color coordinated, with an inside remote control for the driver's side and a convex surface on the passenger side. The idea with the latter touch is to help eliminate the Corvette's traditional blind spot. To forestall confusion in looking from one side mirror to the other, a cautionary notice is printed on the convex surface.

One other tiny touch struck me as I stepped toward the car. The color coordinating seemed to have extended even to the radio antenna, which was black with a little red tip on it. But it wasn't until I'd climbed in and buckled up that I realized the reason for the unusual antenna. It was designed to receive three different kinds of signals—AM, FM, and CB—and when I reached for the shift lever I noticed the CB mike clipped down on the console just to my right. It's a complete in-dash package that will be available in January for about $500. A variation on the theme, also new this year, is an AM/FM/tape player combo. Unfortunately, the packaging does not yet permit all four functions.

As departure time drew near, McLellan pointed out a few other new items inside the cockpit. The most important of these is the steering column, which has been shortened

two inches and can accommodate a tilt/telescope wheel option. Both these features help immensely in the ease-of-access/egress department. The steering column lock has been changed from the complicated back drive linkage previously employed to a simple key release lever setup, and my car also had a new optional sport steering wheel. Corvette buyers are sure to love the latter, a padded three-spoke leather-wrapped number that allows an unobstructed view of the speedometer and tach in all positions.

To the right of the speedo and tach, five lesser gauges—water temperature, fuel, clock, oil pressure, and voltmeter (replacing the old ammeter)—are clustered, aircraft style, at the top of the redesigned center console. With the exception of the clock, all are nicely visible, and a low-fuel warning light now augments the setup. The electric window switches have been relocated from their former position on the hand brake housing to a handler spot just below the shift lever.

Another welcome touch for 1977 is the availability of cruise control for the Corvette, its on-off switch mounted inside the steering column tilt control lever, just ahead of the new turn signal stalk, which contains high beam and windshield wiper switches.

Overhead, the Corvette team has further improved rear vision with a new windshield-mounted Donnelley rearview mirror, a special rubber-mounted version designed to defeat vibration.

Some small but welcome touches: new swiveling sunshades, an overhead courtesy light with a brief built-in delay to allow time for map consultation or belt buckling, and a passenger-side coat hook to enhance the always sketchy storage. Another improvement in the latter category is a redesign of the luggage compartment top molding, allowing slightly better access.

Other interior changes are more cosmetic in nature. The leather seats are now available with cloth panel inserts for more comfort, the old woodgrain door panel inserts have been replaced with satin-finish black ones, and color-coordinated floor mats, in four colors, replace the old black rubber.

McLellan ticks off the list of changes with the pride of a kid reviewing some newly completed supertrick model. I turn the key and sit for a moment listening to the growl of the L-82 engine (with its four-barrel and 9:1 compression, it rates at 210 horsepower at 5,200 rpm, 30 horsepower stronger than the base L-48 version) as McLellan and Jingles grin at me from either side. Then I'm away into the soggy Michigan night to begin living my fantasy during a one-week, 3,500-mile review of the Corvette and its relationship to American motoring.

A journey of that duration naturally produces a substantial amount of adventure, most of it probably too personal and repetitious to share. Like the man said, "You had to be there." However, based on those experiences I'd like to pass along a few general observations.

The thing that struck me most strongly about being a temporary Corvette owner was the effect the car produces in a lot of other drivers, a sort of very temporary insanity. Although I never quite got used to it, I soon came to realize that the guy I'd just passed might very well wind up stuck to my rear bumper, even if it meant he had to speed up substantially to do so; all too often, he'd do the speeding up while I was exposed in the passing lane. The most memorable example of this phenomenon I encountered occurred on a hilly Kentucky trunk highway, where I watched some wild-eyed good old boy in a stake-sided pickup truck careening along perilously behind me for several miles before it seemed worthwhile to bend the speed laws just a little further to leave him behind. And to the Pontiac driver just outside of Corydon, Indiana, all I can say is same to you, fella.

Another thing that made a strong impression on me is the number of Corvette watchers there are out there. I hadn't been in the little café in Straughn, Indiana, for more than 15 minutes before a local bodyshop man came in and asked, "Who belongs to that '77 'Vette out there?" The incident was to recur again and again, even though the identification changes between '76 and '77 are slight.

Corvette camaraderie isn't quite so surprising, except for its near universality; I quickly came to expect a wave or a high sign from drivers of passing 'Vettes of all vintages and was surprised when I encountered the rare lapse, which, interestingly, occurred only among late models. The older the 'Vette, the more I could rely on a greeting from its driver.

Finally, I arrived in Los Angeles with the feeling that Corvettes grow old rather quickly. Even before an unscheduled botanical excursion into the mesquite and sagebrush near Aguila, Arizona, my Corvette seemed in some ways to be approaching middle age. The bodywork had developed several stress creaks, a couple of irritating little rattles had cropped up, the skin of the car showed a large number of mysterious little scuffs and abrasions (presumably these can easily be worked out with a rubbing compound), and I'd managed to collect a surprising amount of tar on the hood and fenders for such a short exposure. Like the scuffs, this too is correctable with a little solvent and elbow grease, but the Corvette's swoopy low snout makes it more vulnerable to this sort of problem than most cars.

While we're complaining, here are a few other considerations, general to the breed and specific to this particular car.

First, while the Corvette is obviously capable of covering lots of ground in short order, it's not the prime piece for cruising the interstates. For the same money you can get a Thunderbird with everything but room service and a lot more living area. The Corvette is probably a lot better for drivers unencumbered by unhandy equipment such as knees. Even though the cruise control frees your legs from the pedals, it's hard to figure out what else to do with them, since the steering wheel severely restricts drawing them up toward your body. The remote control mirror seems to have been designed for operation by the driver's left knee while the right knee crowds the console. Keeping the right leg engaged with the throttle linkage for any length of time is uncomfortable; the angle, limited by the bell housing, is an awkward one, making the cruise control option almost a must.

However, the cruise control is far from being the best in the business. The one on my Corvette was tricky to engage and had a tendency to creep upward in speed at times. It's not a very flexible system and Ford has a better idea.

As has been the case in the past, the Corvette's ventilation isn't able to deal with heat buildup in the passenger legwells, although it's improved this year. I'd hate to own a Corvette without air conditioning, even though it adds over a half G to the ticket ($553).

My car also had a couple of engine peculiarities—a tendency to bog at about 3,500 rpm under hard high-gear acceleration and an alarming thirst for oil—five quarts during the trip to California. The problem with the acceleration flutter seemed at least partially related to altitude; it was most pronounced in the Santa Fe, New Mexico, area (approximately 7,000 feet) and least noticeable at sea level. Fuel consumption was just so-so, ranging during the trip west from around 16 miles per gallon on down in direct proportion to speed, as you might expect. McLellan and friends have been working to cut down fuel consumption but readily admit that fuel economy is a rather low-priority consideration with Corvette buyers. On the *Motor Trend* test loop, our Corvette scored 16.6 miles per gallon.

So much for the carping. Generally speaking, and with the obvious exception of straight-ahead performance, the new Corvette is better than ever. The handling, augmented by a set of fat GR70-15 Firestone steel-belted radials, continues to be equal to almost any challenge (although in the wet, control can depart quite dramatically, as I learned during a scary lesson in hydroplaning in an Arizona downpour). The car stops well, with excellent control, and it takes a substantial amount of speed to get it to slide around much. When you do get it to the throwing-around stage, the balance seems good and the suspension forgiving—in dry weather. There's a certain amount of harshness to the ride, Corvette's trade-off to achieve high-performance handling, but this is to be expected.

Although I never felt that I'd fully mastered the Corvette driving technique, finding myself making minute corrections after I'd already committed myself to a line, these were undoubtedly my shortcomings rather than the Corvette's. The power steering, a standard feature for 1977, is outstanding, with all the road feel one could possibly hope for. The quickness of the steering takes some getting used to in rapid going, but it's precise and reasonably neutral.

Handling, performance, and ride are all last year's Corvette story, however. As McLellan notes, "We're concentrating hard on just trying to keep our performance where it was in 1975 through all the tightening emissions regulations that are coming." Which makes the Corvette story for 1977 one of subtle and positive refinements. Although McLellan privately expresses concern at the Corvette's trend toward boulevard GTism and away from hairy performance, he and his staff are nevertheless honing their product to respond to its market. Their hard work shows to good advantage, inside and out. This may not be the car I dreamed about 20 years ago, but it's still the great American dream machine—with this change: Now it's for grownups.

1977 CORVETTE

GENERAL
Manufacturer: Chevrolet Division, General Motors Corp., Detroit, Michigan
Number of U.S. dealers: 6,030
Warranty: 12 months/12,000 miles
Base list price Point of Entry: $8,647.65
Options on test car:

L-82 350-cid engine	$495
automatic transmission	$146
air conditioning	$553
transparent roof panels	$200
tilt/telescope steering wheel	$165
cast aluminum wheels	$321
AM/FM/CB radio	(price and availability to be announced after Jan. 1, 1977)
Gymkhana suspension	$38 plus various comfort, convenience, and appearance options
	$338

Price as tested: $10,983.65

POWER UNIT
Location: Behind front wheels
Type: OHV V-8
Valve gear: Hydraulic lifters, pushrods, rockers
Bore x stroke: 4.00 x 3.48 in.
Displacement: 350 cid/5,740 cc
Maximum net power: 210 bhp @ 5,200 rpm
Maximum net torque: 255 ft-lb @ 3,600 rpm
Compression ratio: 9.0:1
Recommended fuel: Unleaded
Carburetion: Rochester 4-barrel
Emissions control: Air injection, catalytic converter
Ignition: Pointless high-energy, coil integral with distributor

DIMENSIONS
Wheelbase: 98 in.
Track:
   front — 58.7 in.
   rear — 59.5 in.
Length: 185.2 in.
Width: 69 in.
Height: 48 in.
Ground clearance: 5.7 in.
Fuel capacity: 17 U.S. gal.
Luggage capacity: 7.8 cf

CHASSIS
Body/frame: All-steel frame, fiberglass body
Suspension:
   front — Independent, coil springs, tubular shocks
   rear — Fully independent, double U-joint axle shafts, transverse leaf springs, tubular shocks
Steering system: Saginaw recirculating ball, power-assisted
Ratio: 17.6:1
Brake system: Power-assisted 4-wheel hydraulic
Front brakes: Disc
Rear brakes: Disc
Wheel rim size: 15x8 in.
Tires: GR70 x 15 steel-belted radial

DRIVETRAIN
Transmission: 3-speed automatic
Gear ratios:
   Third — 1:1
   Second — 1.48:1
   First — 2.48:1
   Reverse — 2.08:1
Final drive ratio: 3.55:1
Differential: Ring and pinion
Drive wheels: Rear

TEST CONDITIONS
Weather: Fair
Temperature: 76° F
Altitude above sea level: 950 ft.
Pavement: Tarmac
Test car odometer reading: 4,552

SPEEDOMETER ERROR
Mean velocity error: nil
Odometer error: nil

WEIGHT
Curb weight, full tank: 3,650 lbs.
Distribution, front/rear (%): 48/52
Test weight, half tank: 3,596 lbs.

SPEEDS IN GEARS
Mph/1,000 rpm
First — 8.5
Second — 13.5
Third — 21.0

ACCELERATION
0–30 mph — 3.7 sec.
0–40 mph — 5.1 sec.
0–50 mph — 6.6 sec.
0–60 mph — 8.8 sec.
0–70 mph — 11.5 sec.
0–80 mph — 14.7 sec.
0–90 mph — 17.9 sec.
Standing quarter-mile: 16.6 sec.
Speed at end of quarter-mile: 82.0 mph

BRAKING
30–0 mph — 37 ft.
60–0 mph — 149 ft.
Fade rating: nil

MANEUVERABILITY
Steering wheel diameter: 14.75 in.
Turns lock-to-lock: 2.92
Turning circle diameter: 38.6 ft.
Tire pressures, front/rear: 20/20 psi
Time through slalom: 12.5 sec.

FUEL ECONOMY
Mileage on MT 73-mile loop: 16.6 mpg
EPA weighted average mileage: 17 mpg
EPA city mileage: 15 mpg
EPA highway mileage: 20 mpg

NOISE LEVEL
Interior at idle: 57.5 decibels
Interior under full acceleration: 77.5 decibels
Interior at 30 mph: 67.5 decibels
Interior at 60 mph: 71.5 decibels

1980 CORVETTE

PETER FREY
Motor Trend, October 1979

Some new notes in an old refrain: the legend still sings, but the song remains the same.

IT ALWAYS SEEMS to be the case that, no matter which other more important cars are being introduced, the new Corvette gets much more attention than can be reasonably justified, especially considering that in recent years the process of change has been agonizingly slow, confined usually to the customary cosmetic fiddling and the gradual process of making standard all the equipment that was once optional. This strangled evolution has become so predictable that it is mildly amusing to read the company's press release that describes the changes made to the 1980 Corvette as "major surgery." The visual changes consist of new front and rear spoilers, which are molded-in rather than bolted-on, a deep-set grille with integral parking lamps, and side cornering lights that come on automatically when the headlamps are on and a turn signal is activated. That, along with some new badges, is it.

The front spoiler, to give it proper credit, is a functional aerodynamic device that not only improves the drag coefficient but also scoops up air to help engine cooling. The quest for good aero numbers and the resultant gains in fuel economy also led to a new lower-profile hood.

It became apparent to us that the heavy hand of the Corporate Average Fuel Economy (CAFE) standards had descended on the Corvette just as hard as on every other car and resulted in an engineering effort that pared 250 pounds from the curb weight, bringing it down to 3,519 pounds and dropping it two notches in the EPA's weight-classification scale. Several times during the course of the presentation, high-ranking officials stated that there will be no car in General Motors' product lineup that will be subject to the upcoming "gas guzzler" tax—including the Corvette, which they are fully aware would sell like the proverbial hotcakes, tax or no. The weight reduction program incorporates the application of new lightweight materials and technology. The front and rear bumper systems were redesigned and now have some fiberglass components. Body weight was cut by making the window glass, door skins and the hood thinner, and by fabricating the removable roof panels from a new lightweight, low-density fiberglass. Certain chassis members and support structures have been lightened, and the differential housing and engine intake manifold are cast aluminum.

The drivetrain holds no surprises. In 49 states, the familiar 350-cid V-8 is coupled to a 3.07 rear axle. There is a choice of horsepower, with the standard L-48 or the optional higher-output L-82. Exact horsepower figures have not been finalized but may be expected to be in the 195 and 225 ranges, respectively. These same states will also enjoy the choice of a four-speed manual or three-speed automatic transmission. The California version of the car will, as usual, be available in only one configuration: a 305-cid V-8, automatic transmission, and 3.07 rear axle.

The search for fuel economy also resulted in some changes to the transmissions, with the four-speed getting higher first and second gears, allowing lower rear-axle ratios without unduly compromising low-end performance. The price to be paid is in top speed and upper-range acceleration. The automatic has a new torque converter clutch that, in the drive range, couples the engine's power output directly to the clutch disc and output shaft, completely bypassing the torque converter. This eliminates slippage and parasitic power loss. The clutch automatically engages and disengages above and below 30 miles per hour or when the brakes are applied, all of which reduces drag on the engine and in turn results in better economy. Curiously (due to some emissions-related problem no doubt), the lockup transmission will not be available on California-bound cars.

In terms of standard equipment, the Corvette continues with a list so lengthy and so full of luxury and convenience features that it stands unique among all vehicles to which the term "sports car" is still applied. It includes such things as power steering, power-assisted four-wheel disc brakes, air conditioning, power windows, dual-remote outside mirrors, tilt/telescopic steering wheel, AM/FM radio, built-in anti-theft alarm, T-top, and P225/70R-15 steel radials mounted on 15x8-inch wheels. Also standard are a variety of courtesy lights, a color-keyed interior and—as the result of a half-lunatic indignity—a speedometer that only goes up to 85 miles per hour. The relatively short options list consists of such things as power door locks, rear window defogger, cruise control, glass roof panels, a gymkhana suspension, a variety of radio/tape/CB systems, and aluminum alloy wheels.

Designers have also devised a folding, molded plastic rack that plugs into grommeted holes in the rear deck, between the rear window and tail spoiler. This allows you to stow your removable roof panels externally, leaving the area behind the seats free for the limited amount of cargo you can wrestle through the doors and over the folded-down seatbacks. A good idea, we suppose, but it seems like a damned inglorious way to haul around pieces of your $14,000 sports car.

One of the Corvettes that made a brief appearance at the presentation had a hatchback rear window. We questioned the engineers about the possibility of production, and

The visual changes on the 1980 Corvette consist of new front and rear spoilers, which are molded-in rather than bolted-on, a deep-set grille with integral parking lamps, and side cornering lights that come on automatically when the headlamps are on and a turn signal is activated.

they replied that the idea had been considered but was eventually rejected because the distance someone would have to bend over and reach to install or remove cargo made it impractical. Sounds like pretty thin reasoning to us. The full story undoubtedly involves some aspect of economics, which is a perfectly reasonable consideration, even for one of the largest corporations in the world. With the focus of the market shifting toward less flamboyant, more miserly vehicles, however, the idea of offering at least some semblance of dual-purpose practicality to help offset the negative aspects of owning a specialized, consumptive vehicle seems the most basic sort of marketing logic, if not in immediate profits or increased sales, then at least in the long-term effects of consumer opinion.

Our testing of the Corvette was somewhat limited due to the conditions under which it was made available. The part of the GM proving ground we had access to was the "black lake," a featureless expanse of asphalt so large that you could spin a car at 100 miles an hour and never get close to the edge, and the huge two-lane oval track that surrounds it. During the Thursday session, the two Corvettes were, as always, in great demand, but we finally managed to get behind the wheel of one. There were posted speed limits—and proving ground security people strategically placed to enforce them. The maximum speed allowed was 55 miles per hour, but a few clandestine foot-to-the-floor blasts on an unobserved curve served to prove that the 1980 Corvette still has a fair amount of get-up-and-go, up to about 80 miles per hour, anyway. With no changes to the suspension, the Corvette rides and handles as in previous years, and the four-wheel disc brakes operate with smooth, fade-free efficiency.

We returned early Friday morning, after most of the crowd of journalists had departed, for the instrumented part of the test. The security people obligingly blocked off a section of straightaway for our use, and we made several passes that produced less than dazzling numbers, which we attributed partly to the extreme heat and humidity of the day. An incident then occurred that gave us an insight into the nature of corporate engineering and the effects of cost accounting when dealing with high-volume production. An engineer, who shall remain nameless and whom we hold blameless, stated that he had performed the same test with the same car and had managed significantly better quarter-mile times. We stepped out and offered to let him give it a try. He then made a slow lap around the oval to get the engine cooled down and to get some cool gasoline into the carburetor float bowl. He lined up the car on the straight, revved the engine, dropped the clutch, and the right rear halfshaft U-joint broke, made a tremendous noise, and, with its flailing, dealt a death blow to the shock absorber and various suspension components.

It was later explained to us—by this same engineer, after an inspection teardown—that the failure was caused by human error. In their haste to get the cars assembled for the presentation, the mechanics used a rear-axle assembly designed for an automatic transmission–equipped car. The U-joints were of a lighter-duty construction than those normally installed in manual transmission cars, and that was the reason for the malfunction.

The explanation seems reasonable, but because in the realms of corporate doublespeak, "lighter-duty" equates to "cheaper," it offers some disturbing thoughts about the effects of the philosophy behind it. We can understand the idea of designing a part with just enough strength to meet the expected loads, with a margin of excess able to cope with the occasional overload, but every manufacturer, including GM, is cutting that "over-engineered" margin right down to the bone in an effort to lower costs and save weight. This too we can understand, but it makes us a little nervous to consider the prospect of using a car so designed in the manner that its image and reputation, both carefully guarded and maintained by the company, suggests.

Despite our misgivings, the 1980 Corvette is in fact a Corvette, standing proud, the final survivor of the visionary philosophy of a bygone time. Though there are other cars that now represent a challenge to the Corvette's traditional performance supremacy, none of them look like it, make you feel the same when you drive them, or have the same effect on bystanders. People treat you differently when you arrive in a Corvette. The car's appeal has completely transcended its mechanical capabilities, which are still considerable, and acts directly on the psyche of the buyer. It is still a symbol of manhood and status and is for many the shining goal of a misty dream.

There is a line from an old movie that somehow seems appropriate. A reporter, speaking to a political figure who had just given a revealing interview about his supposedly checkered past, said, "If there's one thing I've learned, it's that when the legend becomes fact, print the legend." Journalistic tactics have changed since then, and we just can't justify that approach, even about so venerable a machine as the Corvette. We will print, however, that although we have a sort of love/hate thing going with the car, it is still a legend, though a legend in a holding pattern. The Corvette is scheduled to be reborn in 1983, heir apparent to all of GM's mega-technology, and though we are happy that it survives at all in this restrictive day and age, we eagerly await its successor, hopeful that it will carry the name to new heights.

The new Corvette includes such things as power steering, power-assisted four-wheel disc brakes, air conditioning, power windows, dual-remote outside mirrors, tilt/telescopic steering wheel, AM/FM radio, built-in anti-theft alarm, T-top, and P225/70R-15 steel radials mounted on 15x8-inch wheels. Also standard are a variety of courtesy lights, a color-keyed interior and a speedometer that only goes up to 85 miles per hour.

CHEVROLET CORVETTE L-82

SPECIFICATIONS

Vehicle type: Front-engine, rear-drive, 2-passenger coupe
Base price: N/A
Options on test car: L-82 engine, 4-speed manual transmission, AM/FM stereo tape player, external T-top panel stowage rack
Price as tested: N/A

ENGINE

Type: OHV V-8, water-cooled, cast-iron block & heads, 5 main bearings
Bore x stroke: 4.00x3.48 in.
Displacement: 350 ci
Compression ratio: 8.9:1
Fuel system: 4-barrel carburetor
Recommended octane number: Unleaded
Emission control: Federal
Valve gear: Overhead valves
Hp (SAE net): N/A
Torque (SAE net): N/A
Power to weight ratio: N/A

DRIVETRAIN

Transmission: 4-speed manual
Final drive ratio: 3.07:1

DIMENSIONS

Wheelbase: 98.0 in.
Track, front/rear: 58.7/59.5 in.
Length: 185.3 in.
Width: 69.0 in.
Height: 48.0 in.
Ground clearance: 4.3 in.
Curb weight: 3,519 lbs.
Weight distribution, front/rear: N/A

CAPACITIES

Fuel: 24 gal.
Crankcase: 4.0 qt.
Cooling system: 21.6 qt.
Trunk: 8/4 cf

SUSPENSION

Front: Independent, unequal-length A-arms, coil springs, stabilizer bar, telescopic shock absorbers
Rear: Independent, transverse leaf spring, lateral struts, control arms, telescopic shock absorbers

STEERING

Type: Recirculating ball, power assist
Turns lock-to-lock: 2.9
Turning circle, curb-to-curb: 37.0 ft.

BRAKES

Front: 11.75-in. discs, power assist
Rear: 11.75-in. discs, power assist

WHEELS AND TIRES

Wheel size: 15x8 in.
Wheel type: Aluminum alloy
Tire make and size: Goodyear P225/70R-15B
Tire type: Steel radials
Recommended pressure, front/rear: 35/35 psi

TEST RESULTS

ACCELERATION

0–30 mph	2.7 sec.
0–40 mph	4.1 sec.
0–50 mph	5.7 sec.
0–60 mph	8.1 sec.
0–70 mph	10.3 sec.
0–80 mph	13.7 sec.
Top speed	N/A
Standing quarter-mile	16.18 sec./85.6 mph

BRAKING

30–0 mph	43 ft.
60–0 mph	182 ft.

FUEL CONSUMPTION

EPA city:	N/A
MT 73-mile test loop:	N/A

SPEEDOMETER

Indicated	30	40	50	60
Actual mph	30	40	50	60

Since engineers have played such a significant part in our story, we shall close by discussing something that one of them said. He mentioned that he wouldn't be surprised if the introduction of the all-new Corvette was postponed until '84 or '85, pushed aside for more important, higher-volume programs. To the managers who make such decisions we say that the Corvette is a Beach Boys sort of a car in a disco-crazed sort of world. The music is good, but it's time to step up the tempo.

THE NEW CORVETTE

KEVIN SMITH
Motor Trend, March 1983

It's an American original, a world-class performer, and a job well done.

I T DIDN'T HAPPEN this way, probably. But it should have. Select Chevrolet person-nel were receiving the assignment of their professional lives, public wants and corporate needs giving the command: Make us a new Corvette. And it had better be good.

A directive like that deserves drama. You remember a certain television character who made a living out of seemingly impossible missions. Now in place of Dave McLellan (chief engineer), Jerry Palmer (designer), and Fred Schaafsma (development engineer), picture an agent of the Corvette group entering an imaginary phone booth, turning on an imaginary tape recorder, and listening to a cold voice set out his team's task.

Good morning, Mr. McPalma. For a generation, the Corvette has been America's sports car. It symbolizes a uniquely American approach to performance and image. Children grow up coveting the Corvette, young adults delight in it, and older drivers keep themselves youth-ful with it. Now the time has come for a new Corvette. It must remain true to tradition, yet expand the name's horizons. It must continue as a fashion leader, but with unrivaled capa-bilities. It must, simply, be the finest performance automobile ever produced in this country. Your mission, and you must accept it, is to create the new Corvette.

Automotive cognoscenti have always had trouble with the Corvette because it has always been an enigma. Two seats qualified it as a sports car—the only one made in America—but it was too heavy and raucous to be embraced by the more effete elements in the sports car crowd. Even the factory was not entirely sure what the Corvette was sup-posed to be, right from the car's inception. Was this a bare-boned sportster, a personal tourer, a high-technology toy—or what?

Corvette fans don't care about any of this. They like the car for what it is, and if it doesn't fit into established categories, well, so much the better. The Corvette has created for itself a unique place in the automotive world. It continues to be an American phenomenon.

Styling is an important part of the Corvette's appeal. Its body shapes—three basic gen-erations with innumerable refinements through 30 years—have always looked modernistic

THE NEW CORVETTE   97

The 1984 Corvette is an honest 140-mile-per-hour automobile.

for their times and completely unlike anything else. Today, a Corvette of any vintage stands out on the street, which makes its owner similarly prominent.

Another Corvette tradition is technical innovation. Through a history that has included big developments (plastic bodies, all-disc brakes) and small ones (hideaway headlights, disappearing wipers), the Corvette has served as a showcase of engineering progress. Features it pioneered have become commonplace on common cars. People expect the Corvette to embody the latest in automotive technology.

Interior accommodation, especially since the mid-1960s, has really set the Corvette apart from the sports car norm: The car is too comfortable and luxurious. Purists are just not marching to the Corvette's beat when they complain that air conditioning and power windows are out of place in a serious performance car.

That's the other ingredient in the Corvette recipe: serious performance. Good power and some effective hardware have long blessed the Corvette with decent performance capabilities. Maybe sophistication and refinement were marginal. Certainly the car has never had the dainty balance of some classic sports machines (most of which it has survived). But in fine American fashion, the Corvette got the job done.

After all the ballyhoo about the coming '83 Corvette, there isn't even going to be one; Chevrolet is calling the new car an '84. But however it's labeled, the new-generation Corvette must live up to some tough standards and meet some high expectations. It has to carry on tradition, be successful in the present, and introduce the future.

The look will be all important. Corvettes have always had futuristic styling. But efficiency must dictate the body shape. The design must penetrate the air cleanly and package occupants effectively. It must also be recognizable. With one look, everyone must know immediately what this car is.

Jerry Palmer's job was to come up with a contemporary shape for the new Corvette, one that would still retain a familiar Corvette face. In the high-security Chevy Studio 3 at GM's Warren, Michigan, Tech Center, Palmer and crew began work on this body in 1978. They tapped a history of ongoing Corvette projects that included the rakish mid-engine show car dubbed first the 4-Rotor (for its Wankel-derived power plant) and then the Aerovette (when a V-8 was substituted).

A ground clearance requirement from the engineers determined how low Palmer could locate the occupants and the design grew outward from there, incorporating various key elements: the windshield rake (at 64.5 degrees from vertical, the steepest GM has ever attempted), the low hood line (made possible by a new front suspension that allowed mounting the engine lower), the sealed nose (it's a "bottom breather," taking air up from the high-pressure area ahead of the front spoiler).

Clean, sweeping lines took shape on paper and then in the wind tunnel. At the clay stage, full-size mockups were taken out onto the pavement and examined in the rearview mirrors of tow cars "to be sure we had that 'move over' look," says Palmer.

Familiar Corvette idioms include the pointed nose, peaked fender lines (though much more subtle now), gill slits behind the front wheels, side and rear window shapes, and the flat tail panel with four large lights. Yet the car is unmistakably different and more modern. Its size is deceiving. All the broad, flat contours give it an expansive look, but it's almost nine inches shorter than the '82 Corvette. It rides on a two-inch-shorter wheelbase. In fact, every dimension measures less than on the previous car except width, which has been upped two inches for improved interior space.

Palmer and his people have enhanced the cleanliness of the new body by "designing to the joint." The rub strip that encircles the car serves as the parting line between major panels, leaving a minimum of other seams. Integration of the tires and wheels also smoothes the look. Because these special Goodyears have been in the program all along, the stylists could blend the body edges right into the sidewalls.

Wind tunnel tests of the new car produced a drag coefficient of 0.34. That's excellent if not pacesetting. Mazda's RX-7 and Mitsubishi's Cordia match that figure, while the new Audi 100 (our future 5000) boasts a 0.30. But note one thing: That amazing Audi number climbs to 0.32 on the high-line Turbo through the simple addition of slightly wider tires (205 section) and a bigger grille opening. On the Corvette, designers had to work with the huge 255/50VR16 tires and the deep wheel housings they require, so the 0.34 CD looks commendable. Also, the two-seat Corvette leaves much less length in which to taper down the roofline and tail than does a car with a back seat. The old Corvette had a CD of 0.44.

With its headlights raised, the Corvette suffers a CD increase of 0.017 rather than a more typical 0.060–0.070. Instead of pivoting through the minimum arc á la Firebird—which pokes the flat, square-cornered covers up into the airstream—the Corvette lights rotate through 167 degrees, completely exchanging the daytime cover surfaces for smoothly faired-in headlights.

Like every Corvette body before it, the '84 is molded in glass fiber reinforced plastic. The supporting structure underneath, however, uses a new arrangement. A galvanized and welded steel uniframe surrounds the cockpit, with extensions reaching fore and aft to carry the powertrain, suspension, and bumpers. Body panels in the cockpit area—the roof hoop, door sills, and dash—are bonded to the uniframe. Other pieces, including the soft facias front and rear, bolt on. The removable roof panel latches at all four corners and comes in a choice of body color fiberglass or tinted acrylic.

Perhaps the most noteworthy body piece on the Corvette is its hood. This is the largest single urethane molding the industry has ever seen. It hinges forward to reveal the entire front portion of the car, for both service accessibility and aesthetics. The '84 Corvette has had its engine compartment styled. Says Jerry Palmer, "We wanted people to see the great hardware, so stylists had access to areas formerly closed to us. We designed the (magnesium) air cleaner and valve covers. We helped locate every hose and wire." It's neat and orderly with lots of pieces worth seeing, such as bright aluminum accessory brackets and suspension arms.

With 280 ft-lb all the way from 1,600 to 3,600 rpm, the engine is a torquer.

Technical innovation must abound. In the American industry, the Corvette pioneered four-wheel disc brakes, fuel injection, plastic body panels, and much more. That trend must continue. The engineering must be more than effective; it must be daring.

Beyond the engine and automatic transmission, there is not a carryover piece to be found on the new Corvette. The new uniframe structure carries all-new suspension. In back is an independent "five-link" system, with each upright located by its fixed-length half shaft, two trailing arms, a lateral link, and a tie rod. Camber and toe are readily adjustable, there is an anti-roll bar, and a fiberglass monoleaf spring like the one introduced in '81 holds everything up.

A similar spring is now used on the front suspension as well, with upper and lower A-arms and an anti-roll bar. Those control arms and the uprights are beautifully forged in 6061 T-6 aluminum and save nearly 36 pounds over last year's parts.

Since 1965, big vented disc brakes have stopped every Corvette wheel. That's still true in the '84, though the parts are new. Sturdy, flex-resistant aluminum calipers by Girlock of Australia grip 11.5-inch rotors. Swept area is actually reduced (to 330 square inches from almost 500) but the new line pressures, friction coefficients, and especially tire traction add up to tremendous stopping power.

Rack-and-pinion steering finally has made it onto the Corvette, with integral power assist. Overall ratio is a quick 15.5:1—and that's on the base suspension. With the Z-51 handling option, it's a lightning-fast 13:1, with a mere two turns of the wheel separating right lock and left lock. Stiffer shocks and springs complete the Z-51 package and help the "preferred direction" Goodyears on 8.5- and 9.5-inch wheels do their best.

Gas-charged Bilstein shock absorbers were being evaluated at the time of our test and will become production items shortly. They offer a little better damping consistency as well as greater resistance to bottoming.

At a claimed 3,150 pounds, the new Corvette weighs more than many hoped it would. Development engineer Schaafsma admits they had aimed for 3,000, but he points out that a 3,150-pound car that works is better than an unsatisfying one weighing 3,000 pounds. We agree, and the 250-pound reduction from the former car is nice. Still, this thing weighs nearly as much as a Camaro, which at 3,300 pounds is itself no featherweight. The Corvette is not out of line with cars like the Porsche 928 (3,285 pounds) or the Ferrari 308 GTSi (3,250); we just would have liked to see all the plastic and aluminum and magnesium give more stunning results.

To move its mass around, the '84 Corvette relies on the L-83 engine introduced in 1982, the 350 V-8 with dual, electronically controlled throttle body injection units on a crossram intake manifold (hence the "cross-fire injection" tag). Its maximum of 205 horsepower comes on at 4,300 rpm. It generates 290 ft-lb of torque at 2,800 rpm, and the curve lies above 280 ft-lb all the way from 1,600 rpm to 3,600, so this is quite a torquer.

Trickery abounds in the engine compartment. A single serpentine belt drives the accessories, the cross-flow radiator has an aluminum core and plastic side tanks, the exhaust system is stainless steel, and the ignition control is electronic and programmed for 91-octane unleaded premium.

Backing up the motor is either the four-speed overdrive automatic (700-R4) from last year or a complicated new four-speed manual with computer-selected automatic overdrive in the top three gears. Speed and throttle position sensors feed data into a black box, which "reads" whether the driver is cruising or pushing hard. When moderate speeds and light throttle indicate gentle driving, an 0.67:1 planetary gear set behind the transmission cuts the ratio reduction in second, third, and fourth for increased fuel efficiency. A heavier foot tells the system to withhold overdrive, or to kick down out of it, and then the box operates just like a normal four-speed manual.

Almost. No computer program can completely anticipate what a driver may want in the way of gearing, and crossing in and out of the overdrive's speed/throttle window can produce unexpected (and perhaps undesired) upshifts and downshifts. The system improves the car's showing in EPA tests (Chevy claims 2.5 miles per gallon in the combined rating compared to a conventional five-speed), but it seems programmed more for that laboratory cycle than on-the-street running.

Whichever transmission is fitted, the entire powertrain is tied together and mounted to the rest of the car in novel fashion. A rigid, cast aluminum C-beam, partially encircling the driveshaft, bolts to the transmission at one end and the differential at the other. This unitized driveline then attaches to the car with only four bolts, two securing the engine mounts to the front crossmember and two holding an alloy wing beam from the differential to the rear frame. The engineers favored this mounting system because it eliminated frame crossmembers within the wheelbase, reducing weight and intrusion on interior space.

The car feels like a precision surgical instrument. Whatever you input to the steering is exactly what you get back.

Progress with continuity: The new Corvette looks especially clean and subtle alongside the '82 model, though its heritage remains unmistakable.

Inside, the car must feel right. That means advanced styling, effective driver information systems, and careful space allotment. It must be pleasant as an environment, yet functional as a cockpit.

Interior space of the '84 Corvette is carefully designed. Shapes, surfaces, and materials are businesslike, as well as pleasing to the eye. There is all the room most drivers could want (with the passenger only slightly cramped in the footwell) and no excess space going to waste. Leg- and headroom are up fractionally over the previous car, and shoulder room across the cockpit is increased a generous 6.5 inches.

Getting into this pleasant place requires some athletics—thanks to the large-section structural rockers, a close dash panel, and high bolstered seats. But it's worth the effort. Even the base seats cradle their occupants comfortably and with adequate support in the lower back and thighs. Upholstery is soft nylon, with a heavy wool layer underneath for breathing and absorption. Moving up to the optional seats adds power adjustments for seat-back angle, torso bolsters, and lumbar support. On the driver's side, in addition, are fore-aft and up-down controls, plus pivoting at front and back. So the array of possible driving positions is truly infinite.

An adjustable steering wheel allows further tailoring of the layout. The column tilts up and down, and a lever just above the hub releases the wheel to telescope in and out.

The only comfort problem that almost everyone will notice is the handbrake lever mounted in the left rocker where it digs into the driver's calf during spirited cornering. Very long-legged drivers may also find the dead pedal too close to allow a comfortably extended left knee.

With such equipment as air conditioning, power windows, electric mirrors, and remote hatch release standard, there is precious little left to make up the options list. Leather trim, cruise control, rear window defogger, and CB radio are about it. Except for the one option no one should go without: the premium Delco/Bose audio system. Similar to the outfits introduced last year in the Toronado, Riviera, Eldorado, and Seville, it has been designed specifically for the Corvette's interior. Its four speakers, with individual equalizers and amplifiers, deliver about the best sound you'll ever hear in this cockpit.

The dash panel is simple and attractive (except for the cushion that sticks out at the passenger like an air bag caught in mid-deployment) with the instrumentation dominating the view. It comprises digital readouts and liquid-crystal graphic displays.

While your ears are tantalized, your eyes are likewise entertained. The dash panel is simple and attractive (except for the cushion that sticks out at the passenger like an air bag caught in mid-deployment) with the instrumentation dominating the view. It comprises digital readouts and liquid-crystal graphic displays. The light show can get fairly spectacular, and while we still fail to see any advantage over old-fashioned round dials, the Corvette's is the first digital panel that we can at least imagine coming to accept. Its design actually makes for decent communication of information, though a glaring sun still washes out the numerals.

Directly in front of the driver is the readout bank, with a large speedometer display on the left, a matching tachometer on the right, and a cluster of minor indicators in the center. The last incorporates a stacked-bar fuel level gauge surrounded by four digital readouts, each of which can be switched between two functions. The two upper gauges give oil temperature or pressure (left) and coolant temperature or volts (right). Each of these has a warning light that comes on if a reading reaches a critical point, and a priority system automatically calls up that reading, even if the gauge is set on the other function at the time. The two lower readouts in the cluster show miles per gallon (instant or average) and trip odometer or range remaining on that tankful. All readings can be shown in either English or metric units.

Integration of the tires and wheels also smoothes the look on the newest 'Vette.

Both tach and speedo combine big digital numerals with stacked-bar graphics to give an exact reading along with an at-a-glance indication. That largely answers some of our complaints about such panels: With a quick look, numerals alone don't give a vivid picture of where you are and where you're going in the rev scale, while a string of lights may fail to provide an exact reading when you want one. The Corvette panel offers both.

A stylized trace of the horsepower curve gives the tach scale its shape, including its pronounced peak just past 4,000 rpm. When working the engine hard and concentrating on the road, the driver can see readily where the revs are relative to that peak. The speedometer graph, shaped like a time/distance acceleration curve, does a similarly decent job.

You may be wondering about the speedometer's range. This is supposed to be a performance car, after all. Rest assured. The liquid-crystal display (LCD) graph runs off scale at 85 miles per hour, but the digital numerals, we are told, can handle 158.

Emissions controls and fuel economy requirements will be no excuse for lackluster performance. Acceleration and top speed must be among the best available today, and chassis response, braking, and cornering capability must set new standards for production cars.

The 1984 Chevrolet Corvette is an honest 140 mile-per-hour automobile. In one of the test cars we drove, on one particular road and one particular day, the speedometer digits showed us 144 (and our fifth wheel later confirmed the speedo's accuracy). A top speed like that puts the Corvette in some pretty select company: Ferrari's 308 GTSi (140), Jaguar's XJ-S (140), Porsche's 928 (140), and 911 (138). The Corvette also leaps off the line with the best of them. Its 0–60 mile-per-hour clockings in the high-6s give it a second or more on all but the lightweight 911, which may edge it by a few tenths. So in terms of raw speed, the new Corvette—emissions equipment, pushrods, iron block and all—is at least the equal of the very fastest cars you can buy today.

And there's more. Its big disc brakes and sticky tires pulled our test Corvette to a stop from 60 miles per hour in 120 feet. That is the shortest distance we have ever recorded for a production car on street tires. The imported names above require from 140 to 160 feet. In performance and casual driving, on both public roads and test tracks, these brakes never call attention to themselves, so perfect are they in pedal effort and modulation, balance, fade resistance, and stopping power. They just slow the car like no other system you can buy.

And there's still more. On a none-too-clean skid pad, the Corvette generated 0.92 g of lateral acceleration. That too is a record for our testing of cars offered for sale to the public. The Ferrari/Jaguar/Porsche crowd groups around 0.75–0.82 g, and our previous best for street tires (if not exactly a production car) was 0.87 from the ERA Cobra replica.

You should be impressed. Especially when price comparisons enter the picture. Chevrolet has not fixed Corvette prices at this writing, but the most informed rumors place them in the mid-20s; under $25,000 for a base car, a couple thousand over for one fully optioned. That will put the Corvette comfortably under all those other cars (the XJ-S and 911 start in the low-30s) and way under some of them (the 928 is $40,000, the 308 $60,000).

But what are you *not* getting for the money you save over the high-priced imports? Aside from intangible qualities like prestige and exclusivity, you may not get construction that feels quite as rock solid. We can't say for sure how regular production units will compare with the early cars we tested, but we did hear more body rattle than we'd hoped for (though clearly less than in the previous Corvette).

Subjective judgments on the Corvette's driving behavior are almost universally positive. Only the 4+3 auto-overdrive manual transmission gets indifferent marks. It's a nice idea that just doesn't work well enough. Accelerating gently on light throttle in second or third, we easily reached the speeds that define the upper limit of the overdrive window (about 40 in second, 50 in third). More than once, we were actually reaching for the lever to make a casual upshift when the transmission abruptly kicked down from overdrive to direct. And throttle adjustments through a long fourth-gear curve can have the transmission shuffling in and out of overdrive, to the detriment of stability. In the end, you wonder why they bothered with all the complexity and expense.

Some refinements to the computer program may rectify the problems, but two other solutions suggest themselves. A switch to lock out overdrive would let the driver choose when he wants it to help. Chevrolet cannot offer a defeat switch without having to EPA-certify the car with defeated overdrive, but we understand there is this little orange wire anyone can snip into.

A CORVETTE FREAK WOULD give his left one for a day like this, I thought. Chevrolet had invited a few of us along for a ride in the new Corvette. Leave the Biltmore in Santa Barbara, up over San Marcos Pass, through the boondocks to Santa Maria, back into the hills after San Luis Obispo, over mountains out into the desert, more mountains and down through the canyons into Ojai, then a little freeway back to Santa Barbara. The only limit your own.

And I had the best seat in the house. From the start to the lunch stop, some 200 miles, I was paired with Dave McLellan, Corvette chief engineer. Without the right connections you couldn't buy a day like this, it ain't for sale. I just lucked into it.

Naturally, I took the wheel first. But after an hour or so, someplace on Foxen Canyon Road, I suggested we swap seats. As much as forming my own impression, I wanted to know what the chief engineer had to say about this new car he had been working on for years, but which had been driven off the safe confines of the GM proving grounds only minimally.

The 46-year-old McLellan was born in Michigan, raised in Detroit, went to school at Wayne State, started with GM in 1959, and has been Corvette chief engineer since the first of 1975, when Zora Arkus-Duntov retired. He's from heartland America, and this is his car. Yet since it's a child of the proving grounds, this was one of its first runs outside the test tube. Up to now, its subjective characteristics had been developed largely in objective terms, and there were reams of graphs and computer printouts to verify the data. But on Foxen Canyon Road McLellan could at last drive his car without all that, and I sensed he was learning at least as much from this trip as I. In no way does his engineer's mind consider this a finished, final product.

When I first saw the bare display chassis, I told him it didn't look American, meaning the forged aluminum suspension pieces and box-section chassis weren't at all like what Detroit has been cranking out for generations. "But it is American!" he said. Barreling along through some California hills, we continued the conversation. He was absolutely right. We've been conditioned by the

Germans to have a mental image of what "high technology" should look like, and the pieces on the Corvette don't really fit that image, either. An aluminum suspension link should be an I-beam section with cylindrical ends for the bushings, according to this conditioning. McLellan said that was about how the first of these Corvette pieces were designed. But through the application of highly sophisticated testing procedures, the engineers made the rear trailing links with a round cross-section, tapering outward smoothly into bushing ends, because it's significantly stronger that way, they learned. It doesn't look conventional American, but it doesn't look German, either. It looks new and is truly of a higher technology than that which has conditioned conventional thought on the subject. We've all known GM had more automotive engineering knowledge than anybody else, it just wasn't applied very elegantly. But on Dave McLellan's new Corvette, it is. This might well be the highest-technology car in the world, and it's American, every inch of it.

All this came clear at something over twice the national speed limit through the California boondocks, 200 miles in a new Corvette with its chief engineer, each of us learning something we'd save for later. In the afternoon, with another terrified passenger, I sailed McLellan's new Corvette across the desert with its digital speedometer registering somewhere in the stratosphere. I'll save that, too, but the best part was the morning. Like I said, days like that ain't for sale. You can't buy them. Only live them.

— Don Fuller

Alternatively, a buyer can just order the excellent automatic transmission. It's a fine mechanism, with four forward speeds, 0.70:1 overdrive in top gear, and a lockup torque converter. It delivers firm upshifts and immediate downshifts. What more could you want? Stirring the cogs by hand is still fun, but over a twisty, unpredictable road, this automatic could well be faster than the manual box. In instrumented testing, we found the automatic's handicap to be virtually nil even in straight-ahead acceleration (0.1 second in 0–60, 0.2 in the quarter-mile). With an automatic this good, it's hard to justify a manual that doesn't always follow orders.

Happily, the chassis follows orders through just about anything. The '84 Corvette sticks and snakes over a winding road the way you imagine a not-too-old Can-Am racer would. Its stability makes for unruffled 55- and 60 mile-per-hour cruises over mountain roads signed for 35. Only miserable road surfaces challenge the chassis and only at twice the national speed limit or better.

Never has a Chevrolet product carried a price tag this high, but never has the company— or any U.S. carmaker—built a vehicle so good in so many ways. It will surely attract people who never considered a Corvette before, even as it's embraced by longtime Corvette fans. All the qualities it needed to have, it has in great abundance. Stylish appearance? Obviously. Fresh engineering? Just look. Proper comfort? But of course. Formidable performance? Stand back.

There may be no better way to see the U.S.A. Mission accomplished.

FORMULA ONE CHEVY: A TECHNICAL OVERVIEW
OF THE WORLD'S BEST-HANDLING PRODUCTION CAR

Visualize a room full of high-level General Motors engineers and managers. The year is 1978 and the subject is the next-generation Corvette, specifically its handling dynamics. There are some rolled-up sleeves, loosened ties, shirt pockets full of pencils, and many personal calculators. There are not feet up on the table or chairs leaned back.

Some very heady names are being thrown around as targets—Porsche 928, Ferrari 308, Datsun 280ZX, Porsche 944. Data from these exotics will be used to establish what a good handling car really is. How it corners, brakes, accelerates; how it handles at high speeds (120 miles per hour plus); and the most elusive of all criteria, how it "feels."

But engineers don't talk about how a car feels; they talk about esoterics like yaw response, roll gain, transient response characteristics, and lateral acceleration. The target cars were to be analyzed and the numbers used as a baseline against which the new Corvette would be held accountable. At meeting's end, that was the charter: design and build the best.

The '84 Corvette is the best-handling production car available in the world today, regardless of price. There is no questioning this statement; it is a demonstrable fact. The real question is this: how was it accomplished?

Very early in the development phase of the program, Pirelli 225/50VR16 P7 tires were used for evaluations. The GM engineers chose them because they were the best and largest available at that time and a good starting point. Initial evaluations showed the P7s to be a little soft (no pun intended) in a couple of performance areas, and the Goodyear people were asked to meet the Corvette engineers' requirements. Since the tire contact patch is where all the action happens, that is where chassis design really begins. The tire design group was asked to concentrate on improved tire life, better wet traction, and reduced rolling resistance, without compromising handling, transient characteristics, or high-speed capabilities.

The result is the new Goodyear "Gatorback" P255/50VR16, the only V-rated original equipment tire in the United States, and the first 50-series production car tire from Goodyear. The unique unidirectional tread pattern (a direct descendant of the company's Formula One racing program) is responsible for excellent wet traction capabilities of the tire. The tire generates a 10 percent increase in wet traction over the standard Eagle GT pattern, attributable to its

continued on next page

continued from page 106

22 percent increase in contact patch area at 62 miles per hour (100-kph standard wet traction test). To reach the mileage rating bogey, a deep tread (12/32 inch) was used to achieve the 40,000-mile target. Some special trickery was needed to get the necessary tread stability at high speeds, and the result was a nylon belting structure, circumferentially over the steel belt, which controlled growth at high speeds. After switching to the Gatorback tread design for reasons of wet traction, the engineers were pleasantly surprised to find the tread pattern actually quieter than the Eagle GT pattern.

Corvette designers were busy developing a wheel for these tires and the result is also a first: the widest wheels ever available on a production car in the United States and possibly in the world. The rear wheels are 9.5 inches wide and the fronts 8.5. In addition, the wheels have unidirectional vanes that pump air over the brakes, and the combination of different widths front and rear and different vanes right and left means that a given wheel will only fit on one corner of the car. This obviously requires GM to inventory four times as many wheel/tire units and is indicative of the Corvette group's dedication to this car's excellence.

The ultimate tire is of little value if the suspension system cannot keep it in correct contact with the road. In addition, the wider the tire contact patch, the more critical it becomes to maintain the optimum contact. The function of the suspension system is to maintain this optimum tire contact with the road while the sprung mass (all the vehicle and occupants supported by the springs) goes through the many possible combinations of pitch, roll, and yaw. This is a complex requirement. Corvette engineers first concentrated on the location of the major components of the car with the goal of achieving the lowest possible center of gravity. A low cg reduces lateral weight transfer while cornering and longitudinal weight transfer under braking and acceleration and allows softer springs and anti-roll bars to achieve the same degree of roll control. Attitude control in high-cg cars requires higher-rate springs with attendant ride harshness penalties.

Another parameter critical to roll control is the vertical location of the roll center. Independently suspended cars typically have the front and rear roll centers at different heights, so it is more accurate to consider the roll axis (imaginary line connecting the front and rear roll centers) and its relationship with the center of gravity. The vertical distance from the roll axis to the cg is the moment (lever) arm on which the centrifugal force acts; the sprung mass then rotates about the roll axis. Corvette engineers have juggled the height of the roll axis to minimize the absolute value of the moment arm, and the real-world effect of this is excellent roll control without the harshness normally associated with such low roll angles. When driven at its limits, the Corvette develops amazingly low roll angles. The cornering speeds are very high, and even though the driver is aware of the high centrifugal forces at work, the car seems almost perfectly flat. This phenomenon of low roll at high cornering power is what engineers call "roll gain," and the accompanying chart compares the '84 'Vette with some of the target cars.

One characteristic that definitely qualifies in the area of "feel" is yaw response. If yaw response sounds like a letter from an Alaskan moose, not to worry; it is simply more engineerese describing how the vehicle reacts to steering inputs. The yaw axis extends vertically through the roof of the car at its geometric center. While cornering (viewed from above) a vehicle rotates about this yaw axis and its rotational speed is the yaw velocity expressed in degrees per second. When moving in a straight line, the vehicle's yaw velocity is zero, and yaw response is a measure of how quickly it reaches the steady state yaw velocity after a steering force is input. When the driver turns the steering wheel, many things take place: clearances in the steering system are taken up, suspension bushings deflect, tires deflect, and (finally) the vehicle rotates about the yaw axis. The vehicle oscillates slightly as it settles into the steady state yaw velocity (even though no further steering is input). This oscillation (decay in engineerese) is critical to the feel of the car and received

concentrated attention from the Corvette engineers. The accompanying charts show these concepts and again compare the Corvette with the target cars.

In terms of real-world driving feel, a high decay time might best be described as "twitchiness," resulting in a vehicle that would wiggle around as the driver turned into a corner. The '84 'Vette, with its extremely low decay time, feels like a precision surgical instrument. Whatever you input to the steering is exactly what you get back from the car. Approaching a corner (at any speed) requires you to wait until the precise moment, put in the exact amount of steering lock, and the car goes absolutely where you have aimed it. No fiddling with the steering wheel is needed; it just goes zap and you are through, looking to the next. How fast is it through turns? Engineers measure a vehicle's cornering capabilities by running around in a circle (hmm, wonder if that's significant) called a skid pad. It is a method to measure steady-state cornering velocity, and its associated lateral acceleration is expressed as a percentage of gravity (1 g is 32.2 feet per second). A vehicle that achieves a speed equaling 16.1 feet per second around the skid pad would therefore have a cornering "speed" of 0.5 g. Many factors affect a vehicle's cornering capability: weight, cg height, roll couple distribution, track/wheelbase dimensions, and (perhaps most important) tire/wheel combinations. An accompanying chart compares the cornering speed of the cars, and shows the clear superiority of the '84 'Vette in this category.

Engineers use the skid pad method of measuring cornering speed because of its objectivity. When done correctly, it effectively eliminates the driver from consideration. It is possible to tune the car to perform well on a skid pad at the expense of other areas of handling, but this is not the case with the new Corvette. In all other handling criteria, the 'Vette is exemplary, and the high values of lateral acceleration are truly representative of the car's capabilities.

The Corvette group's pursuit of excellence has introduced new technologies not previously known in the corporation. Some results are forged 6061 T-6 aluminum suspension members, new lightweight aluminum brake calipers, and gas shock absorbers that will show up as a midyear change across the board. As reported in the road test, the Corvette's braking distances are phenomenal (generating approximately 1.2 g of longitudinal deceleration) and illustrate the efforts by the group. The brake calipers are Australian, the rotors American, and the friction material Japanese. This combination of suppliers was necessary to meet the braking requirements of the design group and no compromises were allowed. If this policy meant some ruffled feathers in the corporation, well then, so be it. The result was considered more important than maintaining the status quo, and the leaders went to bat to get these critical items for the car.

Is the '84 Corvette the perfect high-performance handling car? No, far from it. It is definitely overweight, and the rear suspension is its Achilles' heel from a chassis dynamics standpoint. It is, however, the best-handling true production car you can get your hands on, with no qualifiers. And remember, this is the first production year for the car. The overweight problem can perhaps be dealt with over time: as chief engineer Dave McLellan explained, the designers felt it was better to err on the high side in this first model. The resulting thicker skin, heavier-gauge materials, and generally heavier components tend to get incorporated permanently, in our experience, but we'll give them the benefit of the doubt at this point. The rear suspension shortcomings (high camber change) can be overcome with some design changes as the model progresses, and indeed future efforts to further lower the cg height would benefit the presently high rear roll center. A lower cg would allow the engineers to lower the rear roll center to (reduce jacking effects), while still maintaining the excellent roll gain characteristics of the 'Vette.

As you will appreciate as you read through this issue, it is difficult to be critical of this newest Corvette. Its handling dynamics are second to none. It will get better, of course, but presently it represents a very high level of technology, and we have driven many a fully developed race car that would give anything to handle as well.

— Ron Grable

'84 CHEVROLET CORVETTE

SPECIFICATIONS

GENERAL

Vehicle mfr. . . . . .Chevrolet Motor Div., General Motors
Corp., Warren, Mich.
Body type 2-passenger, 2-door
Drive system . . . . .Front engine, rear drive
Base price . . . .$24,000 (est.)
Major options on test car Automatic transmission Z-51 handling
package, Delco/Bose stereo, power
adjustable seats
Price as tested . . . .$26,500 (est.)

ENGINE

Type . . . . .V-8, liquid cooled, cast-iron block
and heads
Displacement . . . . .350 ci (5,733 cc)
Bore x stroke . . . . .4.00x3.48 in. (101.6x88.4 mm)
Compression ratio 9.0:1
Induction system . . . . .Electronic injection, dual throttle body
Valvetrain . . . . .OHV
Crankshaft . . . . .Cast iron, 5 main bearings
Max. engine speed . . . . .4,500 rpm
Max. power (SAE net) . . . . .205 hp @ 4,300 rpm
Max. torque (SAE net) . . . . .290 ft-lb @ 2,800 rpm
Emissions control . . . . .EGR, 3-way catalyst, oxygen sensor
Recommended fuel . . . . .91 RON unleaded

DRIVETRAIN

Transmission . . . . .4-speed automatic
Transmission ratios
(1st) 3.06:1
(2nd) 1.63:1
(3rd) 1.00:1
(4th) 0.70:1
Axle ratio 3.31:1
Final drive ratio 2.32:1

CAPACITIES

Crankcase . . . . .4.0 qt.
Cooling system . . . . .14.5 qt.
Fuel tank . . . . .20.0 gal.
Luggage . . . . .17.9 cf

SUSPENSION

Front Independent, upper and lower A-arms,
transverse plastic monoleaf spring,
Bilstein gas-filled shocks, anti-roll bar
Rear Independent, trailing arms, lateral
struts, adjustable tie rods, transverse
plastic monoleaf spring, Bilstein
gas-filled shocks, anti-roll bar

STEERING

Type Rack and pinion, power assist
Ratio 13.0:1
Turns, lock-to-lock 2.0
Turning circle, curb-to-curb 40.1 ft.

BRAKES

Front 11.5-in. vented disc, power assist
Rear 11.5-in. vented disc, power assist
Swept area 329.9 sq. in.

WHEELS AND TIRES

Wheel size 16x8.5 in., 16x9.5 in.
Wheel type Cast alloy
Tire size P255/50VR16
Tire mfr. & model Goodyear Eagle VR50
Tire construction Steel-belted radial

DIMENSIONS

Curb weight 3,150 lbs.
Weight distribution f/r, % 51/49
Wheelbase 96.0 in.
Overall length 176.5 in.
Overall width 71.0 in.
Overall height 46.9 in.
Track, f/r 59.6/60.4 in.
Mini. ground clearance 5.0 in.

CALCULATED DATA

Power-to-weight ratio 15.4 lbs./hp
Brake swept area to weight ratio 209.5 sq. in./ton
Speed per 1,000 rpm in top gear 32.3 mph
Top speed 144 mph
Drag coefficient 0.34

SKID PAD

Lateral acceleration 0.92 g

FUEL ECONOMY (mpg)

EPA rating 16/28

MAXIMUM LATERAL ACCELERATION

(measured on 216-foot diameter skid pad)
CORVETTE Z-51 .95
FERRARI 308 .80
PORSCHE 928 .79
DATSUN 280ZX .75
CORNERING SPEED (in g's)
0.6   0.7   0.8   0.9   1.0

TEST RESULTS

ACCELERATION
0-30 mph . . . . .2.32 sec
0-40 mph . . . . .3.41 sec
0-50 mph . . . . .5.12 sec
0-60 mph 6.96sec
0-70 mph . . . . .9.41 sec
0-80 mph . . . . .12.68 sec
0-90 mph . . . . .16.51 sec
0-100 mph . . . . .23.13 sec
Standing quarter mile 15.42 sec/87.5mph
Passing time   (40-60 mph) 3.55sec
(50-70 mph) . . . .4.29 sec

MPH: 0-70, 0-60, 0-50, 0-40, 0-30
SEC. 0 5 10 15 20 25 30

SPEEDOMETER
Indicated 30 40 50 60
Actual mph 30 40 50 60

BRAKING
30-0 mph 31ft
60-0 mph 120ft

HEAVY BREATHER! CORVETTE ZR-1

RON GRABLE
Motor Trend, October 1988

Chevrolet puts an all-new engine in its top-of-the-line 'Vette.

PICTURE THIS: It's your favorite restaurant, with your favorite date, and you slide up to the valet stand in your new ZR-1 Corvette. It's identified only by a subtle badge on the rear, but this teenage valet is hip—a car junkie—and he *knows* what it is. He's so anxious to get behind the steering wheel, he completely forgets about opening the door for your girlfriend, and hovers by your door instead, waiting to jump into the driver's seat. You tell your concerned date it's okay for him to park it (or whatever else he'll do) because you've engaged the "valet" function, and the poor guy will only be able to get reduced power from the engine.

The heart of the new ZR-1 Corvette clearly beats under the hood. Sure, there's other leading-edge technology aboard, but it's mostly there to accommodate the LT5 motor. The six-speed manual, monster tires, dual-mass flywheel, etc., etc. just wouldn't be necessary except to handle the power and torque coming off the end of the crankshaft. And it comes off in prodigious amounts. How does 300 ft-lb of torque at 1,000 rpm sound?

This engine was the outgrowth of a number of programs, which took place during the early '80s in the Corvette engineering group, ostensibly to determine power levels and engine configuration for future-generation 'Vettes. There was a twin-turbo V-8 program, where it was easy to establish almost any power level desired (a couple turns of the boost screw), in which a total of 12 cars were built for evaluating driveline and handling. Another program involved a normally aspirated 350-ci V-8 of some 600 horsepower configured to see what would be required of the chassis and brakes at prolonged high speeds. In addition, Chevrolet used showroom stock endurance racing to probe the durability and absolute strength limits of individual parts, and the large Repco brakes found on current models are one example of higher-capacity, more durable parts that were a direct result of that racing program.

In addition to establishing the power levels for the future 'Vette, these programs allowed the engineers to identify some definite no-noes. First, they realized the engine for

Year-by-rear development at Chevrolet has upgraded the brakes and wheels to the point where they are now capable of dealing with the awesome speed potential of the ZR-1.

the new 'Vette would have to be a V-8 (this was important enough that Corvette chief Dave McLellan confided they would even have stretched the wheelbase if necessary). Only a V-8 would be acceptable from a smoothness and tractability standpoint, and data from the turbocharging programs told them it would have to be normally aspirated. Turbocharged fuel efficiencies, and emissions, fell short of the position GM wanted for the Corvette with respect to the gas-guzzler issue, and, equally important, turbocharging did not represent the "world technology" management wanted for the corporate flagship.

To capture this world-technology image, outside design firms were contacted and asked to bring their proposals to Chevrolet for an engine project. At this point, Chevrolet was comfortable with the chassis' ability to handle almost anything conceivable from a production motor, so what they were looking for from the engine was a quantum leap in performance: an engine that would stretch the production-car performance envelope to the limit. In the initial thinking stages, no power targets were even established. What Chevrolet wanted was an engine that would push current technological boundaries, one that would lead the way for other manufacturers and an engine worthy of occupying that space between the 'Vette frame rails—after all, there've been some great engines in there. In spring 1985, Tony Rudd of Lotus proposed an engine that seemed capable of meeting all the targets; GM approved and the LT5 was born on the drawing boards of Lotus Engineering.

With current technology, an engine displacing 5.7 liters easily produces 400 horsepower at 6,000 rpm. The real challenges come in producing that sort of power level reliably, while maintaining civilized characteristics for everyday use. Lotus men were given some demanding parameters by Chevrolet engineering chief Fred Schaafsma. First, this was to be unequivocably the best-performing production car in the world. Second, tractability must be at least equal to that of the current car, ditto fuel economy, and, fourth, the engine had to fit in the existing car (difficult because on the assembly line, the engine is mated to the vehicle from the bottom up, through the frame rails, requiring that the new engine be no wider than the old).

One important point made frequently by GM people is that this is not a Lotus engine. It was a joint effort, with the specifications coming from powertrain chief engineer for V-8 passenger cars, Roy Midgley, who was responsible for making sure the finished product met all Chevrolet's requirements. We can imagine the problems that must have surfaced during the project—besides the language barrier and the Atlantic Ocean. The facts that the engine is now a reality, that both sides are still talking to each other, and that the performance is everything expected of it speaks to the amount of cooperation from both sides.

A view of the ZR-1's dashboard.

Producing 400 horsepower from 5.7 liters isn't difficult; everything else being in place, just use a large enough throttle to flow the correct amount of air. Do that, though, and the engine probably wouldn't even run at 1,000 rpm. At low throttle settings and engine speeds, the air velocity through the large throttle would be slow and difficult to modulate. So, to meet Mr. Schaafsma's tractability goal, an innovative intake system was designed incorporating the best of both worlds (large throttle for maximum power and small throttle for low-speed controllability). This airflow system is the keystone to the engine and is responsible for its extremely useable power band. Three airflow sensors (with individual throttle plates) feed into a cast aluminum plenum, where 16 individual intake runners deliver the fuel/air mix to the cylinders, one runner for each intake valve. In the secondary runner for each cylinder, a throttle valve is fitted, which is controlled by the engine computer. All 16 runners have an individual fuel injector nozzle, also answering to the engine computer.

Three airflow sensors (one small, about the size of a quarter, the other two elliptical, approximately the area of a coffee cup) and the electronic control module (ECM) manage the amount of air supplied to the engine. In low-demand situations, all the air is supplied by the small throttle plate; the other two remain closed. Using just this small throttle, the engine produces up to approximately 30 horsepower, good for 90 miles per hour. With such a small diameter, large changes in throttle angle have a small effect of total flow area, so manifold pressure excursions are minimized with the desired high degree of throttle response and sensitivity. In this configuration, we have a large engine breathing through a small throttle, ideal for clean, sharp throttle response, and good torque, because of the high air inflow velocity.

As demand increases, the system clicks into stage two, where the two elliptical throttle plates open. But, as long as the engine speed stays below 3,500 rpm, the computer keeps the butterflies in the secondary intake ports closed and their injectors off. Using all

The heart of the new ZR-1 Corvette clearly beats under the hood. Sure, there's other leading-edge technology aboard, but it's mostly there to accommodate the LT5 motor.

Standard equipment with the ZR-1 option is the ZF six-speed manual transmission.

three throttle plates, the engine produces almost the same power as the current L-98 V-8 (245 horsepower). Incidentally, this configuration is what the valet gets, by virtue of a key-lockable switch.

Now for the serious stuff. When the computer sees full throttle, engine speed above 3,500 rpm, and a falling manifold pressure, it knows it's time to quit fooling around . . . the man up there needs it all. The driver's doing all he can with all three throttle plates open, so the computer bangs open the secondary intake butterflies and brings those eight injectors on line. Now it's all happening; the engine is using all 16 intake valves and all 16 injectors, spinning over 7,000 rpm, and producing almost 400 horsepower. Since these secondary ports and injectors only function at high power demand, they are sized accordingly, being slightly bigger than the primary ports. In addition, the cam lobes for the secondary valves have 20 degrees more duration than the primary lobes for better high-speed power. The engineers had some initial concerns about the effect of the secondary port, while its butterfly was closed, because, even though the butterfly remains closed, the valve continues to open and close. Their concern was what effect, if any, there would be on turbulence and mixing in the combustion chamber. At this point in the development cycle for the engine, no discernible effect has been noticed, but, according to the project people, more work in this area may be necessary.

Previously, the airflow sensors on 'Vettes used the mass airflow system of measurement. This new LT5 intake uses speed-density measurement, in which the computer takes the data for manifold pressure, rpm, temperature, and throttle position to go to an algorhythm table and "look up" the correct fuel/air ratio. Chevrolet chose the new method for reasons of reduced flow restrictions but additional advantages include simplicity and reliability.

Ian Doble, general manager of Lotus Engineering, feels that, no matter how sophisticated the intake system, power and efficiency goals won't be met without the correct combustion-chamber configuration. Combustion stability and speed are critical, so the components are arranged to promote good mixing and turbulence in the chamber. Inflow from the intake valves and the squish properties of the piston and cylinder head combine to achieve this, and the centrally located spark plug reduces the distance the flame front must travel to complete combustion. Heat is quickly removed from the surrounding real estate by the highly conductive aluminum and the close proximity of water passages. The extremely high 11.25:1 compression ratio is indicative of how good this combustion chamber is. In addition, the engine will accommodate lower octane fuels, as low as 90.

A narrow 22-degree included angle for the valves and small-diameter drive gear for the DOHC cylinder heads help keep the width of the engine down so it can fit through the existing frame rails. Included in the head design is a provision for oil to drain back into the sump during hard cornering, a welcome addition for a vehicle designed to produce over 1.2-g cornering power.

The block is cast aluminum and uses forged aluminum liners with Nikasil coating. This method should prove deadly reliable in view of Porsche's success with the process. The block is split at the crank centerline, to which is bolted an aluminum girdle with cast-in-place nodular iron main bearing caps. The girdle is held in place with no fewer than 28 bolts (two dedicated to each main bearing cap), which forms a rigid support for the crank and stabilizes the lower block

Visually, the only differences between the current Z51 option and the ZR-1 are in the rear, where the ZR-1 has a softer, more rounded look, horizontal hash marks across the square taillights, four square exhaust pipes peeking out of the indentation in the bumper, and, of course, the subtle ZR-1 badge.

area. The oil pickup is cast integrally with the aluminum sump, and a sheet-metal windage tray is used to control oil slosh, no mean feat in a vehicle with this cornering ability. Additional development is still underway in the area of oil slosh, as the engineers are not completely satisfied with the present setup.

The crankshaft and connecting rods are forged steel. The oil pump is driven from the front of the crank, and the ignition timing is taken from the crank center to eliminate torsional inaccuracies. Crank journals are 70 millimeters larger than those on the L-98 crankshaft, to deal with the additional power.

The LT5 uses four ignition coils, each handling two cylinders and firing every revolution of the crank, controlled by an expanded version ECM (static timing is no longer adjustable). The new ECM allows a more accurate match of fuel and spark requirements, and with the correct calibration in the module, a nonlinear relationship is possible between fuel, throttle, and rpm. The result of the new-generation ECM is more flexibility in calibrating for horsepower and economy. The timing ring on the crank center also establishes timing for the sequential fuel injection. As many elements as possible were located in the engine V underneath the intake plenum: starter, ignition coils, air conditioning compressor, and alternator. The compressor, alternator, power steering pump, and water pump are all driven by a single serpentine belt.

Also new for this engine is the manufacturing location—Mercury Marine in Stillwater, Oklahoma. MM has been associated with GM for years in converting automotive engines for marine use and probably leads the industry in aluminum casting production and machining. The anticipated volumes for this engine (initial rates of 28 per day with total capability of 50 per day) are in line with MM's experience. MM will dedicate a portion of its Stillwater plant to LT5 assembly, establishing a

The ZR-1 doesn't have the visual impact of a Countach or Testarossa, but it should blow 'em into the weeds without even raising its oil temp.

"clean-room" environment for the purpose, and each engine will be run on a "wet" dyno (running under power with fuel). Most engine assembly lines only turn the finished engines from an external power source to check for componentry leaks and other possible problems.

There's a rumor circulating to the effect that a nickel, placed on edge on an LT5 plenum will remain there, while the engine is cycled on the dyno, between idle and 6,000 rpm. Sounds a little too good to be true, but it's a fact that special attention is given to balance for this engine. All reciprocating parts are assembled in matched sets, and final balance spec is tight, at 0.5 inch-oz. A critical customer will probably just be able to notice a 1.5-inch-oz. imbalance.

Standard equipment with the ZR-1 option is the ZF six-speed manual transmission. To handle the increased torque output of the LT5, the distance between the input and output shafts was increased by 12 millimeters over the L-98 four-speed manual. One unfavorable result of this was an increased clunking and clattering (increased gear backlash), when torque reversals occurred, so the engineers came up with a dual-mass flywheel. Functionally, one flywheel mass is attached to the crankshaft and one to the transmission, with a viscous coupling between. This should effectively preload the engaged gear sets to eliminate backlash.

Included in the transmission shifter assemblies are "blocker" solenoids, which can alter gear selection. If the computer sees the 1-2 shift begin when vehicle speed is between 12 to 20 miles per hour and throttle position is less than 25 percent, it blocks second gear

This is the second Corvette I've illustrated for *Motor Trend* magazine. The first, in the March '83 issue, was done from photographs and drawings of rough prototypes. This time, I have the advantage of looking in the studio parking lot for reference. No, I don't have a ZR-1. I drive a current Z-51 coupe, and this is as close as anyone can come for the moment.

The "King of the Hill," as it was nicknamed during development, is built on a reinforced Z-51 chassis, and there are more similarities than differences between my mere mortal Corvette and the ZR-1. But those differences elevate it into the automotive stratosphere.

The view and perspective of *Motor Trend*'s cover illustration were chosen to highlight the LT5 engine, the focal point of both the artwork and the actual car. The external styling cues that identify the "King" are far more subtle. Corvette-spotters will have to look for the ZR-1's convex rear fascia to catch its identity. This body is also three inches wider than a standard car at the rear wheel center-line, to accommodate the 315/35ZR-17 rear tires. But this blends in with a taper that starts at the forward edge of the doors and is so carefully handled that the job of showing off the extra width goes almost entirely to the new rear fascia.

Looking at the car from the rear, everything says wide, with horizontal slashes on square taillights and square exhaust tips, further reinforced by a much wider license plate recess. All this visually turns the extra three inches into at least a foot.

Starting at the front of the car, under the skin, things change from under-stated to outrageous, with a massive air cleaner mounted to a cooling air duct. This allows the larger radiator to be fitted into the same space as the one for the standard engine. The LT5 also fits into the same space as the L-98, with only minor firewall modifications, despite the normal increase in bulk associated with double overhead cam engines. A narrow included valve angle and place-ment of the head bolts under the camshafts keep the cylinder head unusually narrow. The four camshafts are driven by a double-row roller chain shown instead of the expected Gilmer belt with its much larger pulleys. This allows the engine to be physically smaller, so the Corvette's hoodline remains unaltered. Most of the external accessories are grouped between the cylinder block valley and the bottom of the plenum chamber. Both the alternator and air condition-ing compressor are mounted here, directly beneath the throttle body. These accessories, along with the power steering and water pumps, are driven by a single serpentine belt. A direct coil ignition module mounts at the back, over a specially designed Delco-Remy-Nippondenso gear reduction starter. This starter location leaves the lower sides of the crankcase clear, allowing catalytic con-verters to be incorporated directly into the two tubular exhaust manifolds. One of these can be seen through the front tire in the illustration.

The location of the engine control module (ECM) has also been changed from the standard car, where it was located behind the instrument panel. The ZR-1's expanded ECM can be seen in the illustration directly above the battery, and the new ZF (skip-shift) six-speed transmission can be seen through the ECM and brake booster diaphragm. This transmission, along with the new high bolster seats, will be an option available on all '89 Corvettes.

To see a car of this rarified high-performance level made in America and available to such a large number of enthusiasts makes this project dou-bly exciting for me. The ZR-1 is an honest sports car that has its impact on the road rather than on Rodeo Drive, something that can make any owner "King of the Hill."

—David Kimble

and allows the transmission to engage fourth instead. With the torque available at low rpm, it probably won't have much effect on acceleration, and the window in which the computer intervenes is a low-demand situation anyway. It certainly smacks of Big Brotherism, but was done to boost EPA figures and help avoid gas-guzzler fines.

Chevrolet can point to the Repco brake system on the ZR-1 as a direct development of its showroom stock racing program; you know, racing improves the breed. When Corvettes first entered SS endurance racing (1985), their brakes were woefully inade-quate. Year-by-rear development has upgraded the brakes and wheels to the point where they are now capable of dealing with the awesome speed potential of the ZR-1. The 17-inch wheels allow larger-diameter (read capacity) brake rotors and stiffer dual-piston calipers (front only), while the Goodyears are responsible for some impressive handling performance. The current Z-51 option 13-inch front and 12-inch rear rotors will be used on the ZR-1.

Visually, the only differences are in the rear, where the ZR-1 has a softer, more rounded look, horizontal hash marks across the square taillights, four square exhaust pipes peeking out of the indentation in the bumper, and, of course, the subtle LT5 badge.

The customer willing to cough up the extra money for the killer motor (we don't know how much extra yet) will have to be content in the knowledge that he has the most sophisticated, highest-tech, fastest, best-handling production car available in the world today. It doesn't have the visual impact of a Countach or Testarossa, but it should blow them both into the weeds without even raising its oil temperature. For any nonbelievers out there, we'll arrange a test as soon as possible.

CHEVROLET CORVETTE COLLECTOR EDITION

JACK KEEBLER
Motor Trend, May 1996

The best of the last

DON'T PURCHASE a '96 Collector Edition Corvette and squirrel it away in a warehouse hoping it will make you wealthy. If you want to collect something that really might make a fortune someday, try stamps, dolls, hood ornaments, or a limited run of Elvis plates. Just don't let us hear that you've got one of these road weapons poly-bagged in an Arizona garage. This car was made to be driven. We know—we slipped the wrapper off ours and took it out for a thorough workout. Verdict: This $44,209 (as tested) ragtop is a keeper and is likely one of the best all-around Corvettes ever hatched out of the Bowling Green, Kentucky, plant.

Our test vehicle was ordered with all the go-even-faster stuff: high-winding 330-horsepower LT-4 version of the 5.7-liter V-8, slick-shifting six-speed ZF manual, and the order-code "F45" real-time damping system to tame its track-ready suspension, and low-profile 17-inch tires.

Ironically, the '96 collector edition isn't a limited run (not like the dozen '71 454-ci LS-6 Corvettes built with the ZR-2 race suspension). Chevrolet will build about 5,000 of these special models to celebrate the fourth-generation Corvette's final year of production. That's good, because if all goes according to plan, the significantly redesigned C5 Corvette will be a production reality this December.

Ever since the first Polo White inline–six-powered example was sold in 1953, it's been almost impossible not to notice a Corvette, particularly one in your rear-view mirror. But the collector edition's understated exterior modifications and exclusive Sebring Silver paint make this about as close to a stealth Corvette as its wedge profile, fat rubber, and hunkered-down stance will allow.

Without question, the first thing drivers and passengers notice about the collector edition is its absolutely sparkling engine performance—not just the peak 330 horses of its LT-4, but also its gobs of torque, improved smoothness right up to its 6,300-rpm redline, and rock-steady idle.

"We're sending a message with this engine," explained Dean Guard, project manager for the LT-4. "It says we're strongly committed to OHV engines and the small-block V-8. And believe me, we haven't played all of our cards yet." (The unplayed cards are looking like a new family of sophisticated 270- to 330-horsepower/under 5.0-liter OHV small blocks.)

Guard said his group did three things: They increased durability, "gussied up" the engine bay, and went after rpm because they wanted more airflow—all within a very tight, undisclosed budget.

The 30 extra horses came from classic hot-rodding tweaks like opening up the cylinder-head ports, adding bigger valves, and stuffing in a hotter camshaft with increased lift, duration, and overlap. Electronic multiport fuel injection takes the place of the dual quads that were part of the 'Vette's first "PowerPak" upgrade in '56, but the rest of the mods are well-traveled hop-up territory.

The transmission often defines the difference between good and great sports cars. The Corvette is a great sports car; even with this engine's shaft-warping torque, the ZF six-speed allows short-throw, trigger-quick shifts with just the tips of your fingers and a gentle nudge of your palm. We snapped the shifter back at redline from first, revved to the top of second, and arrived at 60 miles per hour in just 4.9 seconds. You can talk about the good old "big-block" days, but when *Motor Trend* originally track tested a '67 (L71) 427-ci Corvette roadster, it took 5.5 seconds to make the same 0–60 run. Our late-model brute also stomped down the quarter-mile in 13.3 seconds at 107.6 miles per hour; that's ZR-1 territory.

Chevrolet selected a subtle Sebring Silver paint scheme and ZR-1–like wheels for this special edition. Its performance nears ZR-1–levels.

Nevertheless, enjoyable driving in the collector edition doesn't have to be a marathon of stoplight speed runs. One of the really pleasing features of this deep overdrive six-speed transmission is how the engine idles quietly at highway speeds in those very tall cogs, turning barely more than a fast-idle rpm at 55 miles per gallon, in sixth gear.

Nudge 'er up to 65 miles per gallon (1,600 rpm) and the fuel-economy gauge indicates a rock-steady 25 miles per gallon—not bad for a fire-breathing V-8. The EPA gives the LT-4 'Vette a 17-miles-per-gallon rating for the city and 25 on the highway. Drive briskly, though (and you will), and those numbers will plummet fast.

Proper sports cars also need a tight, quick steering gear. This car has one. Its power rack-and-pinion system allows smooth cornering, but with relatively high effort, which is entirely appropriate. The turning circle is still a bit wide, due to the inner-fender clearance requirements of the fat front tires, but the car still can change directions so rapidly and precisely it's as if the steering were hard-wired to the driver's brain.

No Corvette of 30 years ago could pull anywhere near 0.91 g's of lateral acceleration or slice through our 600-foot slalom at 65.7 miles per hour like the collector edition does.

Darth Vader cockpit styling belies the friendly nature of the big, readable gauges and large, well-located controls. The highly bolstered seats feature a unique headrest stitching.

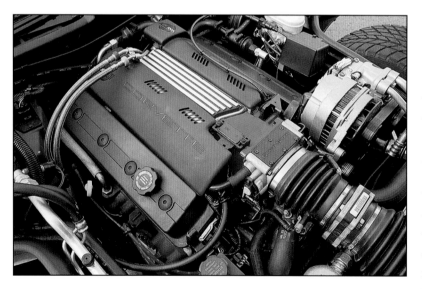

Splashes of red and a "Grand Sport" badge indicate that this 5.7-liter generates 330 horses. Use them all and you'll be blazing to 60 miles per hour in 4.9 seconds.

Normally, this kind of grip completely rules out a reasonable ride, despite the sophistication of independent rear suspension that's been a part of the Corvette's mechanicals since 1963, but, mercifully, Corvette engineers have found a software solution to their harsh-ride headaches.

Our car came equipped with the $1,695 F45 selective real-time damping system. Get it. Yeah, it isn't cheap, but if you're planning to drive this Corvette regularly, it's well worth it to have a far more intelligent system than the FX3 three-way-adjustable shock absorber system that's been available for many years. The F45 setup delivers a range from compliant to quite firm. Rotating the center-console knob to "TOUR" doesn't turn this rocket into a Buick Park Avenue with DynaRide, but it does make a big difference since the markings for "SPORT" and "PERF" could more accurately be labeled "Harder" and "Hardest."

Thanks to the huge Goodyear Eagle GS-C tires and the massive four-wheel anti-lock vented discs, this Corvette is one of the shortest-stopping production cars in the world. At the track, the collector edition used just 119 feet of tarmac to halt from 60 miles per hour.

Once hunkered down in the 'Vette's high-sided bucket seats, you'll notice the black instrument panel. Day or night, it's pure fighter-plane gothic, sort of a cross between an F-18 and the fiery lair in Mary Shelley's classic novel. The bright orange-yellow digital speedometer flickers up with the slightest accelerator movement, but mash the gas in any of the lower gears and the thrust is so fierce the numbers jump in groups of four or five miles per hour rather than making a smooth transition up the scale. Readouts for coolant temperature, voltage, oil temperature, and oil pressure can be displayed one at a time on the

CHEVROLET CORVETTE COLLECTOR EDITION

GENERAL/POWERTRAIN
Body style 2-door, 2-passenger
Vehicle configuration . . . . .Front engine, rear drive
Engine configuration . . . . .90° V-8, OHV,
                                                    2 valves/cylinder
Engine displacement, ci/cc 350/5737
Horsepower, hp @ rpm, SAE net . . . . .330 @ 5,800
Torque, ft-lb @ rpm, SAE net . . . . . .340 @ 4,500
Transmission . . . . .6-speed manual
Axle ratio 3.45:1

DIMENSIONS
Wheelbase, in./mm 96.2/2,424
Length, in./mm 178.5/4,534
Base curb weight, lbs. 3,360
Fuel capacity, gal. 20.0
Fuel economy, EPA city/hwy., mpg . .17/25

CHASSIS
Suspension, f/r . . . . .Short and long-arm, mono-leaf spring,
                                                    anti-roll bar/independent, five-link,
                                                    mono-leaf spring, anti-roll bar
Steering .Rack and pinion, power assist
Brakes, f/r . . . . .Vented discs/vented discs
Wheels, f/r . . . . .17 x 8.5/17 x 9.5, aluminum alloy
Tires, f/r .255/45ZR-17/285/40ZR-17,
                                                    Goodyear Eagle GS-C

PERFORMANCE
Acceleration, 0-60, sec. 4.9
Quarter-mile, secs./mph 13.3./107.6
Braking, 60-0, ft. 119
Slalom, 600 ft., mph 65.7
Skidpad, 200 ft., lateral g 0.91

PRICE
Base price $37,225
Price as tested $44,209

speedo face by pushing a dash button. Somewhat oddly, four analog gauges to the right of the speedo report the same info. To the left, there's a needle-style 8,000-rpm tachometer.

The word filtering out of the Corvette engineering inner sanctum is that the "old car" handled well enough, stopped short enough, and was easily quick enough. In fact, the all-new '97 version may not exceed, or perhaps even match, its predecessor's performance. But what has to be fixed is the current car's tendency to squeak and rattle. Like many Corvettes we've driven, our collector edition's ability to remain squeak-free seemed highly dependent on ambient temperature and humidity. On one 22-degree Michigan morning, the car squeaked and creaked as if the rear hatch area were made of styrofoam. The next morning, over the same roads but 10 degrees warmer, the Corvette's interior was nearly silent.

Unwanted sonic intrusion aside, the collector edition is a car for serious enthusiast drivers. So please, if you're one of the 5,000 or so who get their hands on one, don't flat-bed it home with zero miles on the odometer and keep it stored in a bag of nitrogen for a future payoff. Drive it like its designers intended. Pop the top. Take it out on the road. Put the pedal down and celebrate. **MT**

Without question, the first thing drivers and passengers notice about the collector edition is its absolutely sparkling engine performance—not just the peak 330 horses of its LT-4, but also its gobs of torque, improved smoothness right up to its 6,300-rpm redline, and rock-steady idle.

1953

Only 300 'Vettes were built in its first year; all were powered by a 160-horse Blue Flame six.

1955

Saved from the grave by a dose of power, the Corvette received the 265-ci small-block V-8 in '55.

1957

The new optional Rochester fuel-injection system produced one horse per cubic inch—283 in total.

1963

The completely new Sting Ray had all-independent suspension and an available "split-window" coupe body style.

1965

The 396-inch big-block V-8 produced 425 horsepower. Four-wheel disc brakes debuted in '65.

1967

A favorite of collectors, the '67 L88 427 V-8 slammed out an underrated 430 horses.

1969

New in '68, the Mako Shark–derived Stingray remained in production through '82. The last big-block was used in '74.

1990

The four-cam, 32-valve ZR-1 blazed new high-tech territory and made 405 net horsepower in its last years ('93–95).

'97 CORVETTE

C. VAN TUNE AND JACK KEEBLER
Motor Trend, February 1997

Inside and out: the best sports car America has ever produced

FIRST OFF, KNOW THIS: We were not prepared to like the new Corvette as much as we do. From all the spy photos and inside info we were able to obtain (and scoop the world on) over the past several years, we knew the '97 model would be the most "all-new" car in Corvette history. Not even the original '53 'Vette had as many unique, Corvette-specific parts as does the '97. Nonetheless, our jaded journalistic sensibilities had us expecting a car with far less refined manners and significantly lower levels of overall improvement.

We were wrong. Flat wrong.

From the all-aluminum 5.7-liter LS-1 OHV V-8 and rear-mounted transaxle to its incredibly rigid backbone frame with hydroformed steel side rails, the latest Corvette also is the greatest Corvette. Its power and sound say "pure American muscle machine," its handling is slot-car precise, and—the biggest surprise of all—its ride quality, quietness, and interior comfort rank right up there with German machines in the $60K class. *Refined* isn't a word you could legally use to characterize any Corvette to come before, but it's an entirely appropriate description of the '97.

This is the first all-new Corvette in 13 years. *Yeah, 13 years.* Back when the '84 C4 (Corvette, fourth generation) debuted, the car biz was substantially different from what it is today. That year, Ronald Reagan was still in his first term of office, Chevy was hawking its 1.8-liter diesel Chevette, Chrysler was barely getting its feet wet with minivans, and Ford was still two years away from introducing the first Taurus. In today's aggressive automotive product cycle, 13 years is an eternity, making the previous-generation ('84–96) 'Vette one of the oldest platforms still in production at General Motors.

You'd probably imagine the Corvette to be the multinational automaker's sacred cow, fat with engineering money and backed by executives with unwavering support, but that ain't exactly so. During its lifetime, the model referred to as "America's only true sports car" has been perilously close to death several times. In fact, this C5 model

Dynamically, the '97 is slightly quicker than the C4, handles significantly tauter, and rides about 1,000 percent better.

was originally scheduled to debut in 1993, but a series of severe budget cuts, timing setbacks, and narrow escapes from the hangman's noose ultimately relegated it to the '97 model year.

It's therefore not only amazing that the new Corvette is so great in so many ways, but it's a miracle the car exists at all.

Forty-four years ago, almost to the month, a breathtaking new type of American car was unveiled to the public. The venue was the glamorous traveling road show known as the General Motors Motorama—a huge display of dream cars rolled out before panting audiences from sea to shining sea. There, in turquoise and coral paint schemes, with rocketlike fender shapes and vast acres of chrome was GM's vision of our automotive future.

The overwhelming favorite among the glitzy cadre was a white two-seat ragtop called Corvette. Named after a British fighting ship, the sexy roadster wore a fiberglass body atop its shortened passenger-car frame. Under the hood was Chevy's best power plant at the time: a rudimentary 150-horsepower inline-six connected to a two-speed automatic transmission. General Motors had no intention of putting the Corvette—or any of its other turntable teasers—into production as-is, but the public response to this youthful sportster was so strong, the automaker had to relent.

Within six months, on June 30, 1953, the first of 300 Corvettes to be built that inaugural year rolled out of a hastily constructed assembly facility in Flint, Michigan, and into automotive history. On July 2, 1992, the one millionth Corvette was produced.

It's at first difficult to appreciate how all-new the '97 Corvette is. "All-new" is a term that's bandied about with reckless abandon among automotive publicity teams, and often means little more than fresh body shaping over the existing powertrain and structure. So, consider this: Of the approximately 3,000 parts that make up the '97 Corvette, only a handful of minor pieces, such as fasteners, are shared with the previous-generation car. In a nutshell, that means the C5 comes to market with a new, more rigid chassis design; a new, more powerful engine design; a new, more commodious interior and cargo bay; a new, more aerodynamic body; and much, much more. About the only thing that isn't new is the price: Chevy insiders tell us it will be remarkably close to that of the '96 model. That's unprecedented in Corvette history.

Corvettes are as much about heritage as about innovation, but that makes it doubly tough to design a world-beating new model. The dilemma of what to

The Corvette goes upscale for '97, with a larger cockpit and a vastly more comfortable ride. Full analog instrumentation, optional dual-zone climate control, and a killer Delco/Bose sound system are only a few of the improvements.

keep, what to dump, and what to resurrect was a brain twister that chief engineer Dave Hill, chief designer John Cafaro, and the rest of the Corvette team wrestled with during every waking moment for the past several years. In-depth surveys of current 'Vette owners demonstrated that the new car must be innovative, yet still "look like a Corvette," while surveys of competitive-model owners told the team unequivocally that the C5 should embody significant changes throughout.

And there are myriad other parameters a new design must fulfill: safety, aerodynamics, ease of manufacture, ease of repair, and bottom-line profitability, to name just a few. All of this makes staying true to heritage that much more difficult.

Take a close look at the Corvette's body shaping and you'll see four decades of styling legacy melding with current innovations. The front end retains hideaway headlights in the theme of those first used on the '63 model, the doors and front fenders are coved in reference to the '56–62 Corvettes (now as engine-compartment heat extractors), the fastback rear glass shape harks back to the '78 (25th anniversary) model, the trademark four taillights trace their heritage to '61, and, of course, the body is fashioned of a composite material, though here it's a flexible sheet-molded compound, rather than conventional fiberglass.

But is it a style that works? The vintage-Corvette owners we invited to our photo session at Lanier National Speedway in Braselton, Georgia, definitely thought so. So did most of the frothy-mouthed Corvette fans who followed us into gas stations and fast-food eateries during our time with the C5. A few spectators thought the front end looked "too much like a Firebird" (Cafaro previously designed the Pontiac Bonneville and Fiero), while others saw more styling cues from the Mazda RX-7 (in the doors), Acura NSX (the rear fenders), and Mitsubishi 3000GT (front fenders and wheels) than they'd prefer.

One thing is for sure: This 'Vette will look hot as a convertible. You'll have to wait until '98 for that one, but it promises to be as structurally sound as the lift-roof '97 and

And although the car again features a steel frame with a plastic skin, the frame and skin are completely new and different. One of the important benefits of the new frame's architecture is more passenger and cargo space. Another is its new rigidity, which facilitates better suspension tuning for quieter cruising, an improved ride, and sharper, but more forgiving, handling.

will include a full trunk, à la the '53–62 models. Rumor has it that one year further down the pike, Chevrolet will release a bare-bones fixed-roof coupe model, priced in the low-$30,000 range. More power is waiting to be extracted from the LS-1 V-8, as well—a good thing, because if this generation of Corvette is in production as long as the C4, there won't be a replacement until sometime around 2010.

Park a '97 'Vette next to a '96, and the differences in scale are astounding. The new car may be only 1.2 inches longer bumper to bumper, but it enjoys a 4.3-inch-wider rear track, 3.0-inch-wider front track, and an 8.3-inch-longer wheelbase. There's more interior head-, leg-, and shoulder room, as well as double the previous car's cargo capacity—up to a gaping 25 cubic feet of area to easily hold a pair of golf bags or a week's worth of luggage for two. And the '97 looks far bigger, especially from the rear. That flat expanse of rear fascia is present to reduce aerodrag, resulting in a body that cheats the wind at a class-leading 0.29 CD. Beneath the license plate in the rear fascia is a cavern that allows followers—and there will be hordes of them—to glimpse the four tailpipes and independent rear suspension.

View the car in profile and note the nose-down rake achieved by the long-hood/short-deck design and use of 275/40ZR-18 tires at the rear versus shorter 245/45ZR-17s up front. The sloped hoodline, fast angle of the windshield, and truncated rear fascia are designed primarily to aid aerodynamics, but a welcome side effect is greatly improved forward vision. (The road surface is visible 18 feet closer to the car than in the '96 model.) There's no noticeable improvement at the rear, however, where someone could still hide a battleship in the car's blind spot. Fortunately, the new 'Vette has five mile-per-hour bumpers front and rear.

Open the driver's door to enjoy this thorough redesign's next benefit: improved step-in height. Gone are the days of having to bring along a block and tackle to hoist your bones over the knee-high doorsills. Once inside you'll settle into the comfy and supportive leather buckets. Your companion will revel in his/her newfound lounging area, stretching out into the 6.3-inch-wider footwell thanks to a much smaller center tunnel (another benefit of moving the transmission to the rear). There's a real glove box, a shallow center console, and a nicely integrated dash-top grab handle reminiscent of the '63–67 models.

A superb arrangement of analog white-on-black instruments greets the driver, replete with a fantasy-evoking 200 mile-per-hour speedo, a 7,000-rpm tach, and fuel, oil pressure, coolant temp, and voltage gauges all riding in a diorama-like setting that makes them appear to be on different planes. Turn on the key and everything ramps up to full redline tilt in a diagnostic check, while the night visage delivers a better light show than the aurora borealis. Directly beneath the gauges is a digital display for scanning readouts of 12 functions (typical fuel-economy and trip-computer stuff plus a real-time tire-pressure monitoring system for all four tires). After you've read the directions a few times, you probably can get the system to change the messages to Spanish, French, or German, and even defeat the daytime running lights. Dual-zone climate control is offered for the first time in a Corvette, as is a high-output 252-watt Delco/Bose sound system with a 12-disc CD changer.

The cockpit design is definitely driver-oriented, but without a fervent hormone-raging boy-racer look that would cheapen the effect. Benefiting from one of the best alchemy recipes of form-follows-function and generously ladled-in comfort, the C5's interior is far superior to that of any other Corvette.

The C4's pain-in-the-butt, tools-and-temper-required, heavy lift-off roof panel has been banished to the hell-fired damnation it deserved and has been replaced by a lighter, magnesium-framed roof panel that quickly affixes or releases via three latches and can be whisked out of the cargo area by anyone with more upper body strength than a garden slug.

Don't look for a spare tire; there isn't one. Goodyear's Extended Mobility tires are standard and capable of allowing up to 200 miles of highway driving without air. Positive experiences with the optional run-flat tires on the C4 convinced Corvette's engineers that they could do away with the heavy spare tire and jack and instead use that area for cargo space — a typical example of how the designers worked to make virtually everything better in the '97 Corvette.

From stem to stern, if something was too hard, too cramped, too noisy, too shaky, too cheesy, or too obnoxious on the C4, chances are excellent that it's been fixed on the C5.

Looks are one thing and comfort's another. But how does this beast drive? Twist the ignition key, and the LS-1 fires to life with a distinctive tenor: exhaust tuning like that of a Z28 with a tad more bite. On Road Atlanta's twisty, hilly road course, we blithefully

The wheels have been pushed to the corners for an 8.3-inch-longer wheelbase, but only a 1.2-inch increase in overall length.

INSIDE THE AWESOME NEW LS-1 V-8

The LS-1's raw numbers are 345 horsepower at 5,600 rpm and 350 foot-pounds of torque at 4,400. Those numbers' effect on the 3,218-pound Corvette is pure dynamite.

This all-new all-aluminum OHV small-block V-8 is lighter, far more compact, and less mechanically complex than a similar overhead-camshaft design making the same power.

Starting the refinement process, the chain-driven crankshaft has been tucked deep into the center of the engine. Called a "deep-skirt" block, this robust design together with six-bolt main bearing caps and a cast aluminum structural oil pan reduces the amount of engine bending to reduce vibration and noise.

Although the LS-1 shares its cylinder-bore centers with the old V-8 at 4.40 inches, and the displacement is almost the same at 5.68 liters (347.0 cubic inches), the stroke was lengthened to 3.62 inches and the bore was shrunk to 3.90 inches (0.1 inch smaller than the LT-1). A smaller bore reduces hydrocarbon emissions, improves block rigidity, and aids in-engine cooling.

Although the aluminum heads still breathe through seemingly conventional pushrod-operated intake and exhaust valves, the system's individual pieces have been lightened and modified with roller lifters and rocker arms to reduce friction. The lower mass allows the system to operate more efficiently and accurately at higher operating speeds.

The intake manifold is made of thermoplastic and is similar in design to that used on Cadillac's 4.6-liter Northstar V-8. The heat-resistant plastic intake runners' smooth interior jets the intake air into the port. The plastic also insulates the air charge in the runners from the power-sapping high temperature of the heads.

Fuel is supplied by a multipoint, sequential fuel-injection system controlled by a drive-by-wire throttle system. Chevy calls it ETC, or electronic throttle control. This setup eliminates the mechanical linkage between the

pedal and the throttle blade, allowing the electronic cruise control and traction-control systems to be integrated into a single controller.

Each cylinder is fired by its own ignition coil located close to the spark plug, ensuring a crisp, strong spark for smoother idle, better overall combustion, and lower emissions. The firing order also has been changed to improve idle smoothness.

Instead of using heavy cast-iron exhaust manifolds, a stainless-steel header system was welded up with an inner and thermal-insulating outer pipe. (A cast-iron manifold would have absorbed heat needed by the catalyst during the emissions-critical cold-start test.)

Future applications of the LS-1 assuredly will include the Camaro, Firebird, and, ultimately, light trucks.

turn off the traction control, rev 'er to 3,000 rpm, and drop the clutch like a deranged 17-year-old. The big Goodyears erupt into smoke as the first C5 allowed for journalist use rampages out of the pits and onto the racing surface. (Driving more like a sane person later on showed that the LS-1/six-speed combination exhibits a slight torque deficit under 2,000 rpm; however, the automatic-equipped cars, due to the torque converter's characteristics, are not so affected.)

The Borg-Warner T56 gearbox provides quick and accurate shifts despite being remote controlled by shift rails and overall feels more precise than the previous car's ZF six-speed. The LS-1's power is ready and willing and by 4,500 rpm takes on a dual-intake type of power increase. We accelerate through a fast right-hand turn followed by a brief pull uphill as we pass 90 miles per hour, then up and over, graze the brakes, and settle into an off-camber downhill corner at 75-plus. No push. No twitchiness. No feeling of impending doom. Let's kick 'er up a notch.

Hunkered down into the seat as the cornering loads build, we maraud through the hilly ess-turns with astounding balance, grip, and control. Road Atlanta doesn't have the straightaways to fully explore the car's 172 mile-per-hour top speed, but we do kiss 135 miles per hour a couple of times on the backstretch.

The sound of the LS-1 at high rpm is very cammy in demeanor and wholly appropriate for this all-new car. The feedback coming from the Magnasteer II tuning is eons better

BODY STRUCTURE SECRETS

One of the dirty secrets about the previous-generation Corvette was how soft its body structure was. And although the car again features a steel frame with a plastic skin, the frame and skin are completely new and different.

One of the important benefits of the new frame's architecture is more passenger and cargo space. Another is its new rigidity, which facilitates better suspension tuning for quieter cruising, an improved ride, and sharper, but more forgiving, handling. And this was done without adding mass: Chevy says the car is between 70 and 100 pounds lighter than the previous iteration and uses 34 percent fewer parts.

Measuring some of the changes tells part of the comfort story. The wheels have been pushed to the corners for an 8.3-inch-longer wheelbase, but only a 1.2-inch increase in overall length. Inside, the C5 has 1.3 inches more headroom, 0.7 inch more legroom, and 1.4 inches more shoulder room than before. Behind the seats, the rear cargo area has doubled to a spacious 25.0 cubic feet and now features a much wider, easier-access opening.

Basically there are nine main parts to the new frame: the two hydro-formed-steel side rails, the front and rear steel bumper beams, the backbone drivetrain tunnel, the cast aluminum front suspension crossmember, the rear cast aluminum suspension crossmember, the welded aluminum cockpit and windshield frame, and the instrument-panel crossmember. The removable top panel, which provides structure when in place, features a magnesium frame for lower weight and greater strength.

The seamless tubular steel frame rails were created using a new GM-developed process that uses high-pressure fluid, a metal-forming die, and what looks like a big exhaust-tubing bender. By forcing several thousand psi of hydraulic pressure through the rails in the dies, a precise form is made from a single piece of steel, replacing the 14 welded-together parts previously used.

Although the rails make a major contribution to the steel skeleton's strength, the actual backbone of the new 'Vette is its stamped-steel drivetrain tunnel. To add strength, the tunnel is closed on the bottom with a steel panel that is virtually sewn on with 36 bolts.

Two of the more impressive Corvette structural features are the one-piece, cast aluminum crossmembers to which the suspension arms are attached. In the front, the steering rack is also bolted to its cast member.

Like the past-generation cars, the sheet-molded compound body panels and reaction injection molded fenders are unstressed and ride attached to the steel skeleton.

Speaking of clever composites, the driver and passenger-area floors are a sandwich of balsa wood between composite plastic panels. Although the team looked at other materials, none offered the low cost, noise attenuation, or strength of the wood.

Also, these dramatically curved pieces of plastic enabled the Corvette to nail a phenomenal 0.29 drag coefficient. That's the lowest drag number for any current production car, with the exception of GM's own EV1 electric vehicle at 0.19 Cd.

The big hidden pieces of plastic in the car are the twin, blow-molded fuel tanks that are located above and just in front of the rear axle. These tanks, connected by a bridge tube, hold 19.1 gallons of unleaded premium for a 500-mile range.

---

than that from the Aurora's version of the same setup, with very quick response and only a little bit of feedback weirdness, but we quickly adapt to it. Ditto the throttle-by-wire; it only acts cranky when you've called the traction control into abrupt action, such as by purposefully applying too much throttle on a wet surface, as it takes a count of three to get back to the business of driving.

It had rained earlier in the day, and there are patches of wet pavement and red Georgia clay runoff to avoid—usually at the corner apex or on a blind section of downhill. Running hard in a C4, Viper, or Z-28 at this track in these conditions, 90 percent of drivers would soon see the world in rapidly changing 360-degree pictures; welcome to the big spin! Although it's far easier to go fast comfortably in a C5 under these treacherous conditions, Mr. Hill and company haven't repealed the laws of physics; they've only tamed the Corvette's response to them. A great deal of credit goes to the Goodyear tires, which deliver excellent wet or dry grip, gradual at-the-limit breakaway, and outstanding ride comfort despite the stiff sidewalls required for run-flat capability. (Goodyear, for the first time, will produce snow tires in Corvette sizes, so the fun doesn't have to end in winter.)

You don't feel it from inside the car, but the C5 has a fair amount of body roll. Don't knock it. That's what the stiffer structure allows you to do: soften the springs for improved ride, while the chassis holds everything together. On the highway, the C5 rides like a sport sedan; on the track, it's a pavement-eater of the highest order, taking a bite at corner entry with a near-neutral attitude and tenacious levels of grip. The rear can be coaxed out at will or held in check through hard braking, over broken pavement, or during goofball antics such as lifting off the throttle in a turn. Our tester was equipped with the base suspension setup, but

WHY A REAR-MOUNTED TRANSAXLE

The Corvette's transmission is no longer bolted directly to the back of the engine. Instead, engineers have moved it into the back of the car between the rear wheels, where it spins a Getrag limited-slip differential that transmits power out to the wheels through half shafts.

The big benefits are obtaining a nearly 50/50 front/rear weight distribution, substantial gains in noise reduction, and an increase in passenger compartment leg- and hiproom. The driver's footwell is more than three inches wider and the passenger's is 6.3 inches wider than those of the previous-generation 'Vette.

The LS-1 engine sends its power to the transmission through a slender metal-matrix prop shaft that spins inside an aluminum torque tube. The torque tube rigidly connects the back of the engine on one end to the front of the transaxle at the other end of the car.

There are two transmission choices: an optional Borg-Warner T56 six-speed manual or a standard GM-built Hydra-Matic 4L60-E electronically controlled four-speed automatic. The C4's ZF six-speed has been discontinued. By the way, this manual retains the CAGS (computer-aided gear selection) skip-shift hardware that forces a shift from first to fourth under light throttle for better fuel economy.

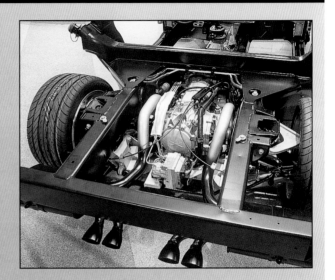

SUSPENSION TRICKS

As in last year's car, the suspension is available in three variations: the base setup, the electronically controlled F45 variable-rate shock-damping system, and the stiff, race-ready Z-51.

Up front is an aluminum short- and long-arm or double-wishbone suspension. The cast lower arms attach to a cast aluminum crossmember. The forged uppers are attached directly to the frame rail. The aluminum arms provide excellent strength with reduced mass for less unsprung weight and crisper wheel control through jounce and rebound. Like the front, the rear suspension is a double-wishbone type, but here both the upper and lower arms are cast.

Forget the spare and jack; all four tires are run-flats (275/40ZR-18 Goodyear Eagles at the rear and 245/45ZR-17s up front). In fact, they work so well that drivers have to be warned about a loss of pressure: the Corvette is equipped with a standard real-time tire-pressure monitoring system that's accurate to within one psi.

The significantly more communicative steering system on the new car is called Magnasteer II. This new rack-and-pinion system, also attached directly to the front aluminum crossmember, varies steering effort electronically by processing vehicle speed and lateral-acceleration inputs.

we did sample the F45 three-way selective real-time damping system on another car and found its tour setting to be most like the base suspension's ride characteristics.

On the skid pad, our tester was good for 0.94 g, with nominal push at the limit; through the 600-foot slalom, it managed an average speed of 66.8 miles per hour, despite near-freezing temperatures and a slightly damp track surface. Nevertheless, 60–0 mile-per-hour braking was recorded in a brief 111 feet. Acceleration testing showed 0–60 miles per hour in 4.7 seconds and the quarter-mile in 13.3 seconds at 106.8 miles per hour. On a dry track, with properly heated tires (and possibly with the F45 or Z-51 competition suspension options), there would be room to improve all those numbers.

On the track, the Corvette proved to be a fire-breathing demon with good common sense—a superfast play toy insured by Mutual of Heaven. On the highway, the car takes on its other personality, that of a cool, refined, long-legged mile-eater—a vehicle you could live with everyday, in a wider variety of weather and road conditions than ever before. With its balsa wood insulated flooring, composed ride characteristics, and virtual elimination of squeaks and rattles, the Corvette has, for the first time in its 44-year history, become a refined, sophisticated, no-excuses-required car. An Olympic athlete instead of a back-alley brawler.

America's most-beloved sports car truly has become world class.

CHEVROLET CORVETTE

GENERAL

Manufacturer . . . . .Chevrolet Motor Div.,
General Motors Corp.,
Detroit, Mich.
Location of final assembly plant . . .Bowling Green, Ky.
EPA size class 2-seater
Body style 2-door, 2-passenger
Drivetrain layout . . . . .Front engine, rear drive
Air bag . . . . .Dual
Base price . . . .$38,550 (est.)
Price as tested . . . .$41,250 (est.)
Options included . . . . .Dual-zone climate control, foglamps,
12-disc CD changer, power
passenger seat
Ancillary charges . . . . .Destination
Typical market competition . . . . . .Dodge Viper, Acura NSX, Porsche
Boxster, BMW Z3 2.8

DIMENSIONS

Wheelbase, in./mm 104.5/2,654
Track, f/r, in./mm 62.0/62.1/1,574/1,577
Length, in./mm 179.7/4,564
Width, in./mm 73.6/1,869
Height, in./mm 47.7/1,212
Ground clearance, in./mm 3.7/94
Manufacturer's base curb weight, lbs. .3,218
Weight distribution, f/r, % 51/49
Cargo capacity, cf 25.0
Fuel capacity, gal. 19.1
Weight/power ratio, lbs./hp 9.3

ENGINE

Type . . . . .90 degrees V-8, liquid cooled, cast
aluminum block and heads
Bore x stroke, in./mm 3.90x3.62/99.0x92.0
Displacement, ci/cc 347/5,680
Compression ratio 10.1:1
Valve gear . . . . .OHV, 2 valves/cylinder
Fuel/induction system . . . . .Sequential multipoint EFI
Horsepower, hp @ rpm, SAE net . . . .345 @ 5,600
Torque, ft-lb @ rpm, SAE net . . . . .350 @ 4,400
Horsepower/L 60.7
Redline, rpm 6,000
Recommended fuel . . . . .Premium, unleaded

DRIVELINE

Transmission type . . . . .6-speed manual transaxle
Gear ratios
(1st) .2.66:1
(2nd) .1.78:1
(3rd) .1.30:1
(4th) .1.00:1
(5th) .0.74:1
(6th) .0.50:1
Axle ratio 3.42:1
Final drive ratio 1.71:1
Engine rpm, 60 mph in top gear . . .1,350

CHASSIS

Suspension
Front . . . . .Aluminum upper and lower control
arms, transverse-mounted composite
leaf spring, 19-mm anti-roll bar
(21.7-mm on Z-51 suspension)
Rear . . . . .Aluminum upper and lower control
arms, transverse-mounted composite
leaf spring, 19-mm anti-roll bar
(21.7-mm on Z-51 suspension)
Steering
Type . . . . .Rack and pinion, speed-sensitive,
magnetic variable effort, power assist
Ratio 16.1:1
Turns, lock-to-lock 2.7
Turning circle, ft. 38.5

Brakes

Front, type/dia., in. . . . . .Vented discs/12.8
Rear, type/dia., in. . . . . .Vented discs/12.0
Anti-lock .Standard
Wheels and tires
Wheel size, f/r, in. 17x8.5/18x9.5
Wheel type/material . . . . .Cast aluminum
Tire size, f/r 245/45ZR-17/275/40ZR-18
Tire mfr. and model . . . . .Goodyear Eagle F1GS
Extended Mobility (run flat)

INSTRUMENTATION

Instruments . . . . .200-mph speedo, 7,500-rpm tach,
fuel level, coolant temp, oil pressure,
volts, digital clock and driver
information system (fuel economy,
tire pressure, trip computer, engine
monitoring, programmable
entry monitoring)
Warning lamps . . . . .Check engine, traction control, ABS,
air bag, seatbelts, door ajar,
battery, security

PERFORMANCE AND TEST DATA

Acceleration, sec.
0–30 mph 2.0
0–40 mph 2.8
0–50 mph 3.9
0–60 mph 4.7
0–70 mph 6.0
0–80 mph 7.7
0–90 mph 9.6
0–100 mph 11.6
Standing quarter-mile, secs. @ mph . .13.3 @ 106.8
Top speed, mph 172*
Braking, ft.
30–0 mph 28
60–0 mph 111
Handling
Lateral acceleration, g 0.94
Speed through 600 slalom, mph . . .66.8 (damp surface)
Speedometer error, mph
Indicated . . . . .Actual
30 30
40 40
50 50
60 60

FUEL ECONOMY

EPA, city/hwy., mpg 18/28
Est. range, city/hwy., miles 344/535

*Manufacturer's data

'99 CALLAWAY C12

JEFF KARR
Motor Trend, June 1998

Inside the 440-horsepower 200-mile-per-hour $140,000 Super Corvette!

ASK REEVES CALLAWAY to tell you the most significant spec sheet number on his new C12 supercar, and it likely won't be the anticipated near 200-mile-per-hour top speed, its 4.2-second 0–60-mile-per-hour acceleration, or its 440-horsepower V-8. More likely the number Reeves will proudly produce is 1998 millimeters, the car's overall width. That makes the C12 just two millimeters shy of the two-meter maximum allowed by international production-based GT2 racing rules. When you've got designs on places like LeMans, this is a big deal.

Overall width is the sort of arcane specification that gets chassis designers all misty-eyed. During at-the-limit cornering (pretty much the only kind that matters at the racetrack), a wider chassis loads all four tires more evenly than an otherwise identical narrow layout. Even tire loading means higher cornering limits and quicker lap times. Callaway's new C12 is right at the maximum width in stock form, increasing its theoretical on-track performance. With clear racing intentions in mind, that puts a two-meter-wide smile on Reeves' face.

Reeves definitely has reason to be happy with the C12. It was one of the hits of the recent Geneva Auto Show, its first public introduction. The C12 is Callaway's crowning achievement in 20 years of producing almost a thousand high-performance vehicles. Another key distinction and the source of considerable pride for this gentleman from Connecticut: To be built by Callaway Cars Europe in its Bad Friedrichshall, Germany, facility beginning this summer, the C12 is homologated and approved for worldwide sale, not as a modification of the Chevrolet product on which it is based, but as a Callaway.

That's a deserved distinction, since so much of the Corvette coupe that serves as the basis of the C12 has been changed or replaced in the elaborate conversion process. In a year of development, Callaway, working with Germany's established IVM Engineering, its partner in this venture, has tweaked, tinkered with, or outright reengineered virtually every system in the car. They'll never recognize the C12 at your local Chevy dealer, or anywhere else for that matter.

A familiar name to Callaway fans, designer Paul Deutschman led the international team that styled the car out of full-scale clay, then digitized the shape and refined it in the computer. On screen, the C12 spent countless hours plowing through computer-generated atmosphere, being tweaked aero-dynamically for drag, lift, and frontal area. Just more than five inches wider than an off-the-rack Corvette coupe (and about three inches wider than a Viper TGS), the C12's proportions look entirely different from the car on which it's based. About all a sharp eye can detect are the shared door cut lines, body-colored door handles, and the greenhouse glass. Even that's been significantly altered in appearance, with the unifying influence of new carbon/kevlar sail panels that move the C12's lines away from the glass-back look of the stock 'Vette. The shape of the lightweight composite body echoes classic sports cars, drafted in a clean, modern style. Rolling on enormous 19-inch wheels wrapped in ultra-low-profile (the rears are the first production-car application of 25-series carcasses) specially developed, run-flat Pirelli P Zeros, the C12 has an ominous presence, tempered with high-tech undertones.

Inside, you'll know it's a Corvette, but the Callaway crew has gone to considerable lengths to make sure that the driver's principal points of contact—and the overall ambience—are pure Callaway. Two-tone leather (coordinated with the exterior color) dresses the bucket seats and the rewrapped steering-wheel rim and airbag cover. The round aluminum-and-carbon-fiber shift knob has a technical look that is forwarded by carbon fiber accents submerged in deep clearcoat on the console, instrument panel, doors, and sills. Should you choose to live out your latent interior decorator fantasies, Callaway offers the possibility of custom—and very elaborate—optional interior upgrades. The sky's the limit—as long as your line of credit holds out.

Such unrepentant luxury is available in the C12 mostly because the car is aimed at an elite and very small group of potential customers who are unaccustomed to compromise and won't tolerate a raw, street-going race car. Today, as he transitions into his 50-something years, Reeves Callaway himself shares that view. As a result, he's worked to ensure the C12 is a refined machine that's driveable every day. He promises a restrained engine note, good suspension compliance, and surprisingly little road noise, given the ultra-low-profile tires.

Just more than five inches wider than an off-the-rack Corvette coupe (and about three inches wider than a Viper TGS), the C12's proportions look entirely different from the car on which it's based.

Those goals were made more attainable, he says, thanks to the latest-generation Corvette's inherent goodness. Instead of repairing weaknesses, the metamorphosis from Corvette to C12 (a process that will take about two months from when a customer places an order) is composed of extending the car's performance envelope, with the help of racetrack-developed modifications and significantly looser purse strings than the Chevy engineers had to deal with.

On the chassis side, Callaway's modifications are driven by the increase in width to two meters. Longer, fabricated stainless-steel upper-and-lower suspension arms move the wheels further outboard and are controlled by Callaway-spec internally adjustable damper assemblies. To dial in the effective spring rates with the longer suspension arms, the dampers wear lightweight coil springs that work in concert with the standard Corvette fiberglass leaf springs. This combination scheme is lighter than going with full coil springing, yet allows for easy tunability by replacing the small coil helper springs or adjusting their preload.

In keeping with the deep-dish racing capability built in throughout the car, the C12 sports new brakes all around to improve stopping power and fade resistance. All four corners have family-size pizza-pan-dimension, 14-inch-diameter, ventilated metal matrix rotors that cut unsprung weight and substantially improve heat dissipation. Specially designed four-piston Alcon calipers grip the discs, with hydraulic pressure modulated by the Corvette standard anti-lock system. All of which is good, whether you're steaming down the Mulsanne Straight at a buck-ninety or screaming into the McDonald's parking lot for a $1.90 value meal.

This sort of added stopping capability matches similar advances under the hood. The latest installment in Callaway's family of SuperNatural engines, the all-aluminum 5.7-liter V-8, kicks out 440 horsepower at its 6,300-rpm peak (up from 345 at 5,600 rpm). Torque

Two-tone leather (coordinated with the exterior color) dresses the bucket seats of the car and the rewrapped steering-wheel rim and airbag cover.

The latest installment in Callaway's family of SuperNatural engines, the all-aluminum 5.7-liter V-8, kicks out 440 horsepower at its 6,300-rpm peak.

has risen from 350 ft-lb at 4,400 rpm, as it rolls out of the Corvette Bowling Green factory, to 395 ft-lb at 5,200 rpm as delivered by Callaway.

According to Callaway, the SuperNatural engine drives much like its Chevy counterpart, but has longer, stronger legs. When the stocker starts to fade slightly at about 5,500 rpm, the Callaway SuperNatural keeps right on charging until it hits the fuel cutoff at about 6,400 rpm—making big, mouth-watering dyno numbers in the process. The bulk of the engine alterations are aimed at moving more air into the power plant, and more spent gases out. Intake-runner lengths have been altered, cylinder head port shapes have been changed, cam profiles redrawn, and the entire exhaust system, including dual catalytic converters, replaced. The pistons and connecting rods are upgraded for periods of high-rpm abuse.

Callaway pegs its C12 performance projections right in the heart of Dodge Viper GTS territory. Initial in-house tests of 0–60-mile-per-hour performance stopped the clock at 4.2 seconds (compared to 4.8 seconds for the stock 'Vette), by virtue of better grip, more power, and almost no increase in weight. The current 192-mile-per-hour predicted top speed (we've heard estimates of up to 200 miles per hour) is about 18 miles per hour higher than the stock Corvette. In this respect, the C12's two-meter width and steam-roller tires work against it by increasing frontal area and, in turn, total drag. The payback comes in maximum cornering power, which should be in excess of 1.0 lateral g (up from 0.93) and overall handling that's even more predictable at the limit than the already exemplary stock Corvette. A full instrumented road test is still a ways off, but our first immersion into the realm of the C12 certainly sounds promising. With final engineering details still to be locked in, production cars won't be available until the fall, so prospective buyers should start saving now. We'll let you know ASAP if it's a true world beater.

So the anticipation builds, heightened further by the C12's limited planned production volume. Something under 40 cars are expected to be built before the end of '98, with a

GENERAL

Location of final assembly . . . . .Bad Friedrichshall, Germany
Body style . . . . .2-door, 2-pass.
EPA size class . . . . .Two-seater
Drivetrain layout . . . . .Front engine, rear drive
Airbag . . . . .Dual

POWERTRAIN

Engine type . . . . .90-degree V-8, liquid-cooled,
  cast aluminum block and heads
Bore x stroke, in./mm . . . . .3.90x3.62 /99.0x92.0
Displacement, ci/cc 347/5,680
Compression ratio 10.3:1
Valve gear . . . . .OHV, 2 valves/cyl.
Fuel/induction system . . . . .Sequential multipoint EFI
Horsepower, hp @ rpm, SAE net . . . .440 @ 6,300
Torque, ft-lb @ rpm, SAE net . . . . .395 @ 5,200
Horsepower/liter 77.5
Redline, rpm 6,450
Transmission type . . . . .6-speed manual
Recommended fuel . . . . .Premium unleaded

DIMENSIONS

Wheelbase, in./mm 104.5/2,654
Track, f/r, in./mm 65.0/1,650
Length, in./mm 191.0/4,852
Width, in./mm 78.7/1,998
Height, in./mm 47.1/1,197
Manufacturer's base curb weight, lbs. .3,263
Weight distribution, f/r, % . . . . .51/4960-0 mph braking, ft.110

Cargo capacity, cu. ft. 24.9
Fuel capacity, gal. 19.1
Weight/power ratio, lb/hp 7.4

CHASSIS

Suspension, f/r . . . . .Upper and lower control arms,
  transverse-mounted leaf springs, coil
  springs,anti-roll bar/upper and lower
  control arms,transverse-mounted leaf
  springs, coil springs, anti-roll bar
Steering type . . . . .Rack and pinion, power assist
Ratio 16.1:1
Brakes, F/r . . . . .Vented disc/vented disc, ABS
Wheels, in . . . . .19x10.0/19x12.5, cast aluminum
Tires . . . . .295/30ZR-19 / 335/25ZR-19
  Pirelli P Zero

PERFORMANCE *

Acceleration 0–60 mph, secs. 4.2
Top speed, mph 192-plus
Lateral acceleration, g 1.00
EPA fuel economy, mpg, city/hwy . . .16/25
* all data estimated

PRICE

Base price $140,000
www.callawaycars.com

The shape of the C12's lightweight composite body echoes classic sports cars, drafted in a clean, modern style.

target of about 150 per year planned when production reaches full speed. Sold on an order basis exclusively through Callaway Cars in Old Lyme, Connecticut (800/231-1121), and serviced through approved centers scattered around the United States, the C12 scores high on the exclusivity index.

The $140,000 base price should also help ensure that you don't see one on every street corner. Building a performance car the way it *should* be built costs money, Reeves Callaway points out. However, he's convinced that, given the C12's capability (and racing potential, should you choose to exercise it), relative to many of the exotics out there, the car is in fact substantially *underpriced*. Clearly, Mr. Callaway is convinced that his new C12 will put a very wide smile on the face of anyone who drives it. About two meters wide, to be exact. **MT**

YESTERDAY & TODAY '99 CORVETTE HARDTOP VS. '69 427 TRI-POWER

JACK KEEBLER AND MATT STONE
Motor Trend, September 1998

Does the newest 'Vette live up to the legend?

1 969. OTHER THAN NEIL ARMSTRONG'S historic walk on the moon and New York's "Miracle Mets," things were tough in the land of the free and the home of the brave. We were a country still reeling from the assassinations of Bobby Kennedy and Martin Luther King Jr. Vietnam was raging, and the Beetles were preparing to break up. But, man, did we have cars.

The daring new Mako Shark-inspired 'Vette was just a year old at the time and still about the hottest hunk of American iron (and fiberglass) on the street. GM's big-block V-8 had grown from 396 cubic inches to 427 back in '66, garnering the affectionate nickname "Rat Motor." It was available in several states of tune, but the coolest of the cool for '69 (aside from the nearly unobtainable L-88) had to be the L-71, rated at 435 gross horsepower and packing three—count 'em, three—two-barrel carburetors. Order us up Three Deuces on a fat block. To go, please.

Fast forward 30 years. Vietnam is long over, and the 'Vette lives. And in C5 form, it may be living better than ever. Chevrolet hinted at several versions of the C5 straight from the get go, and now we have them: the fastback with removable roof, which premiered in '97; the roadster, helping the entire line garner *Motor Trend*'s Car of the Year for 1998; and now, something new again: the "hardtop" coupe. The Nassau Blue Metallic example pictured here is one of the first ones off the preproduction line, and we drove it across the country so it could burn rubber alongside this beautifully preserved, 42,000-mile Cortez Silver '69 427 automatic. We were getting a taste of this newest Corvette during four days at the wheel, driving our featured beast 2,400 miles from its Indianapolis press introduction to our West Coast base.

Something seemed wrong with the traffic headed west on I-40 coming from Flagstaff and going toward Kingman, Arizona. Despite terrific weather, unlimited visibility, and a 75-mile-per-hour speed limit, the vehicles we shared the highway with seemed painted in place on the horizon's canvas. But while those cars, pickups, and motorhomes were laboring up

The Corvette hardtop pictured here is one of the first ones off the preproduction line and was driven across the country so it could burn rubber alongside this beautifully preserved, 42,000-mile Cortez Silver '69 427 automatic.

the mountain grades, our hardtop 'Vette sucked up asphalt like a terrain-following cruise missile on afterburner.

A bit of background on this higher-performance Corvette: Chevrolet's brass had let it slip that a super lightweight, ultra-stripped-down, lower-priced club racer was in the works. But in reality, that's only sort of what we got. Chevy's original concept didn't make a handbrake U-turn; let's just say there was a hard lane change in direction. Although marketing and engineering folks were reluctant to discuss the late changes in specifications, what started out in the original business plan as a much lower-cost, bare-bones version of America's favorite V-8 two-seater has morphed into a slightly more expensive weekend racer's weapon of choice.

So what happened? Better than five years ago, Corvette market planners were conservative about how many could reasonably be sold. Keep in mind that, at the time, Corvette sales were softening, and other powerful competitors like the Toyota Supra Turbo, Porsche 911, and Nissan 300ZX were also faltering badly in the marketplace. A lower-budget version of the C5 was seen as insurance that the Bowling Green, Kentucky, assembly line (which builds only Corvettes) would continue to crank.

Today, every single Corvette is spoken for before it leaves the factory door. So GM financial people asked why they were doing a cheap version of the car that would only squeeze their profit margin. So in a heartbeat, the plan changed. But never say "never": Insiders tell us that, if sales should someday slacken, a lower-budget Corvette could be done quite easily.

The L-88 Corvette of '67–'69 was "done quite easily," too, though probably with a lot less thought—or second thought. Just take the basic 'Vette, stuff in a tire-melting, essentially race-spec 500-horse-plus 427, remove everything that saps power or adds weight, and head for the strip. While this gorgeous 427, owned by Corvette collector M. J. Winer, was not of L-88 spec, it is one of approximately 250 427-cid 3x2s to be equipped with the Turbo-HydraMatic transmission—packing exactly half the gear ratios of the new car's six-speed manual. Other options on our Yesterday Corvette are power windows, steering, and brakes, Positraction rearend, upgraded suspension, AM/FM radio, and the much heralded, but always ignored, speed warning indicator.

Corvette Chief Engineer Dave Hill says the '99 Corvette hardtop was designed to answer the call for a simpler, more fundamental Corvette—something closer to a classic Corvette.

Chevy officials were unwilling to go into exact pricing on the newest variation, allowing only that it will be "the lightest, quickest, least-expensive version of the car." Corvette Chief Engineer Dave Hill describes it: "The hardtop answers the need that's been expressed for a simpler, more fundamental Corvette. But it's one with even more of the performance attributes than the others. And it's the stiffest Corvette of all—12 percent more rigid than the coupe. It's the lightest Corvette [by about 79 pounds] because there's less hardware and glass area. It's also going to be the lowest-priced Corvette of the entire family. But it's no 'stripper.'"

Standard on all '99 Corvettes are four-wheel disc brakes with anti-lock and traction control, electronic throttle control, and run-flat "extended ,obility" tires with electronic tire-pressure sensing, air conditioning, leather seating, power door locks, power windows, heated power mirrors, remote keyless entry, theft-deterrent system, cruise control, and AM/FM stereo with cassette player.

The 427-ci big block V-8 was better known by its nickname: "Rat Motor."

No question, a big chunk of the new car's appeal is its engine. The 5.7-liter LS-1 V-8 with 345 horsepower at 5,600 rpm and 350 lb-ft of torque is the one and only engine offered in all three versions of the car. Not exactly the raging, ground-pounder 427, but probably as powerful given today's more realistic "net" horsepower ratings. And it's way more fuel efficient and environmentally correct.

Our acceleration tests found no difference to 60 miles per hour between this supposedly lighter hardtop and a coupe we tested in our May issue—both took 4.8 seconds. And the quarter-mile times and speed were actually better for the coupe, which ran a 13.2 seconds at 109.3 miles per hour versus the hardtop's 13.3/108.6. But we can attest that today's 'Vettes run quicker once they've accumulated about 3,000 miles, thus the hardtop may be quicker when fully broken in.

On the way across Oklahoma, Texas, and New Mexico, we obtained some incredible fuel mileage, even at a sustained 70 to 75 miles per hour. We never saw less than 28 miles per gallon on a fill. And got a high of 32.5 miles per gallon on one long, fast, mostly

No question, a big chunk of the new car's appeal is its engine. The 5.7-liter LS1 V-8 with 345 horsepower at 5,600 rpm and 350 lb-ft of torque is the one and only engine offered in all three versions of the car.

Taking the classic 'Vette for a spin.

downhill swoop across Arizona. Try that with three two-barrel carbs.

Because Winer's ultra-low-mile, all-original 'Vette came with the caveat of "no hard testing," we used it mostly to gain a feel for how the vintage 427s drove. Fortunately, our forebears had tested a 427 3x2-barrel Corvette in the March '68 issue. Though it was a four-speed/roadster as opposed to our subject '69 automatic coupe, we suspected that test would provide an insight into its mighty, big-block muscle. Well, guess what: Today's heavier, unleaded-gassed, airbagged version would have kicked its fiberglass fanny. The editors of the day achieved a traction-limited 0–60 time of 6.3 seconds in the '68 tester and ran the quarter-mile in 14.1 at 103 miles per hour. Now, that's rolling for sure, no matter the age or era. But in pure terms, the new car just flat outruns the old one, legend and lore be damned.

On the highway, at the border between Nevada and California is a fruit and vegetables inspection pavillion that looks almost exactly like the customs crossings at the international border between Detroit, Michigan, and Windsor, Canada. And as we eased into a white-striped lane, I steeled myself mentally to provide carefully worded responses to virtually any question asked by the huge, badged officer looming outside his booth. But imagine my absolute surprise when he said, "Hang on, there, what are you doing driving this car? You're not C. Van Tune."

My son's jaw dropped open, and I was speechless. How did the inspection station officer know that last statement would have any relevance at all to me? And how would he know if I was or wasn't Van Tune? Had *Motor Trend* alerted California state officials that I was on my way? But wait, I was wearing a blue *Motor Trend* golf shirt with the magazine logo and the *Motor Trend* calipers stitched in white thread. Also, the Los Angeles staff is almost dizzy from high-speed trips to Las Vegas Motor Speedway and more than a couple brain-frying runs through the nearby desert in sport/utes. So perhaps this Nevada station regularly intercepts our editors. But amazingly, this clever guy's next question was almost as impressively insightful.

"Isn't this the new Corvette hardtop?"

Turns out he's also an avid *Motor Trend* reader. I guess I just needed to be reminded that serious car enthusiasts come in all shapes and sizes. And there are even a few who wear badges.

Under the fiberglass skin of its fixed roof, the hardtop's integral all-steel frame is essentially identical to that of the hatchback coupe. But Mike Neal, a Corvette engineer in charge of suspension development, tells us the attached fiberglass roof does bring a large measure of additional overall stiffness to the vehicle.

Chevrolet first offered a fixed-roof Corvette with the '63 split-window Sting Ray. And while this new roof profile is obviously not quite as interesting, it does share the coupe's subtle roof-center declination that's carried quietly into the rear window glass. However, the hardtop will not be the Corvette with the highest top speed. That honor still goes to the hatchback coupe with lowest drag coefficient of the two-seater trio at 0.29.

Backing up our subjective impression, the blue devil wove through our 600-foot slalom with the quickest Corvette pass we've ever recorded, at 68.1 miles per hour. That's significantly better than the Z-51–equipped coupe we recently tested (at 66.2 miles per hour). Along with certain colors, some options aren't available on the hardtop. But Chevrolet's remarkable stability-control system is. This "active handling" system electronically recognizes potentially dangerous oversteer or understeer situations, cuts throttle, and selectively applies all four calipers independently to help the driver maintain control. It's impressive and a safety/handling enhancement well worth considering.

Hardtop versions of the car come with the racing-style Z-51 suspension only. Chevrolet claims this firmly sprung and damped arrangement is designed specifically for "appropriate, sanctioned competitions, or for the driver who desires the ultimate in handling." Usually we'd offer warnings to avoid this type of suspension if you don't intend to drive regularly on a racetrack. But as we drove from Indianapolis back to our Los Angeles office, we found very few road surfaces this car didn't like.

It's in the handling department where 30 years of progress in terms of tire, suspension, and chassis design development really shows. The Mako 'Vette was pretty exotic for its day: Only the expensive, imported brands packed features such as independent suspension and four-wheel disc brakes. The '69 Corvette was an aggressive handler, too, but even then, the nose would go light at speed, the steering lacked road feel, and the

The editors of the day achieved a traction-limited 0–60 time of 6.3 seconds in the '68 tester and ran the quarter-mile in 14.1 at 103 miles per hour. Now, that's rolling for sure, no matter the age or era. But in pure terms, the new car just flat outruns the old one.

Standard on all '99 Corvettes are four-wheel disc brakes with anti-lock and traction control, electronic throttle control, and run-flat "extended mobility" tires with electronic tire-pressure sensing.

whole car felt darty when the pavement got rough. Push is too hard into a corner, and the initial understeer can morph into a big spin of oversteer with anything but perfect throttle control. And the '69's rock-hard bias-ply tires on narrow 15-inch wheels look positively dainty today. But the brakes feel remarkably good and body roll is commendably low, even by current standards.

We've had lots of positive things to say about the C5 Corvette's big, circular analog gauges with their vivid white calibration and the handy digital driver information screen. And, frankly, we see no reason to change a single thing. But Chevrolet has added an optional head-up display system for '99 that projects vehicle speed to 175 miles per hour, an analog sweep tachometer with shift light, and turn signal indicators on the inside of the windshield. The driver can also put bar graph displays for oil pressure, coolant temperature, or fuel level onto the glass. But here again, the head-up system isn't available on the hardtop. No harm there, as we tend to view these systems as little more than gimmicks, and turn them off.

The interior of the vintage 'Vette also feels positively racy, but in a completely different fashion from the '99's. It's leaner, narrower, but more cosseting. The deeply dished, thin-rimmed, three-spoked steering wheel is uncomfortably narrow to handle, and through it you peer into a large 160-mile-per-hour speedo and 7,000-rpm tach. The other gauges are to the right, as are the heater controls, radio, and super-cool fiber-optic monitoring system for head- and taillight operations.

Measuring up the old versus the new.

Styling? The new 'Vette is commanding, standing imposingly on its low-profile rubber, with broad shoulders and a big, muscular butt. But the silver shark is the most captivating. The curves and Coke-bottle waistline are stretched so tightly over the frame, its skin fairly pings when you touch it. So while we're impressed by the looks of the new car, we simply drool over the old one.

Then there's that sound. During the mid- and late 1970s, most cars—even Corvettes—issued forth an impotent, metallic fizz from their catalyzed, fake dual exhaust systems. But the pre-cat, 3x2 427 makes a sharp, slightly cammy, almost manic "plup-plup-plup" that lets you know there's horsepower nearby. Slamming your foot into all three carbs is the automotive equivalent of opening an entire six-pack of beer simultaneously and pouring it into your mouth—nothing but rowdy, bad-boy fun, and to hell with manners. Fortunately, today's engineers have made a spectacular recovery, and the new 'Vette has good chops, too—a reedy intake roar, and deeper, smoother sounds coming from the centrally mounted, four-tip exhaust system.

So which is better? Which should you buy? Which is really the Corvette for a drive across the country—or a trip to the burger joint? There's little question that, if your needs include any sort of real-world driving—a little club racing—the new 'Vette is the way to fly, literally and figuratively. It out-accelerates, out-brakes, and handily out-handles the legendary Mako Sharks, offering carefree drive-ability and palpable gas mileage—as it should, given 30 years of technological and design progress. But for a stylin', you've got to love the tidy shape and 427 cache of the '69. Pull out those T-tops on a sunny day, romp on the gas, and let the three deuces talk to you. The classic 'Vette spews nostalgia from every pore and still honks when you're in the mood. Ideally, you'd buy one of each.

The '99 hardtop coupe is a neat piece. It's lighter, a better handler, and should be cheaper than the already fabulous fast-back C5. It is not the package we anticipated, but it's a good one and will find favor with those who don't care for wind or sun in their hair and who just want the best-handling 'Vette variant available today. The Corvette is still a loud-and-clear definition of American style, two-seater muscle—just as it was in '69. **MT**

REASONS TO RIDE

My almost-16-year-old son and I made the 2,400-mile trip in the 'Vette hardtop from Indianapolis to Los Angeles. Both of us will remember this fast-paced odyssey for the rest of our lives.

Other dads, hearing about it beforehand, would get all misty-eyed or go loud and enthusiastic about road trips they took with their sons. Oddly, most women, with the notable exceptions of my wife and my Detroit colleague, just didn't seem to get it. Why would anyone ever want to drive a car—even a Corvette, especially a Corvette—across the United States instead of flying?

I did it so I could watch my normally late-sleeping boy spring from the bed at 6 a.m. in Clinton, Oklahoma, as if he'd been hit with 5,000 volts, ready to begin another mile-munching day.

. . . so we could stop at a little souvenir shop near Conway, Texas, to buy "Don't Mess with Texas" and "Route 66" T-shirts,

. . . so we could talk and grin about blue 345-horsepower Corvettes and driving fast with some Navajo teenagers at a gas station outside Tuba City, Arizona,

. . . so he could watch me stare down and chase off a would-be spy photographer with a digital camera at the edge of the Grand Canyon who was trying to pop a shot at our 'Vette's abbreviated rear glass and long deck,

. . . so he could lean over the side of Hoover Dam and slowly take in one of the engineering marvels of the twentieth century, a miracle way before NASA was sending men to the moon,

. . . so he could see movie star Martin Sheen cruising beside us up the Pacific Coast Highway near Malibu as the sun was setting.

And most important, I made the trip because when will I ever again get my son's undivided attention for four whole days?

—*Jack Keebler*

CORVETTE 427 ROADSTER (AS TESTED MARCH 1968)

GENERAL/POWERTRAIN
Drivetrain layout . . . . .Front engine, rear drive
Airbag . . . . .None
Engine type . . . . .90-degree V-8, liquid cooled, cast-iron block and aluminum heads
Bore x stroke, in./mm 4.25x3.76/107.9x95.5
Displacement, ci/cc 427/6997
Compression ratio 11.0:1
Valve gear .OHV, 2 valves/cyl.
Fuel/induction system . . . . .Three 2-barrel Holley carburetors
Horsepower, hp @ rpm, SAE gross . .435 @ 5,800
Torque, ft-lb @ rpm, SAE gross . . . . .460 @ 4,000
Horsepower/liter 62.4
Redline, rpm 6,500
Transmission type . . . . .4-speed manual
Axle ratio 3.55:1
Final-drive ratio 3.55:1
Recommended fuel . . . . .Premium leaded

DIMENSIONS
Wheelbase, in./mm 98.0/2489
Track, f/r, in./mm 58.3/59.0/1480/1499
Length, in./mm 182.1/4625
Width, in./mm 69.2/1757
Height, in./mm 47.8/1214
Base curb weight, lbs. 3,425
Fuel capacity, gal, ...20.0
Weight/power ratio, lb/hp 7.9

CHASSIS
Suspension, f/r . . . . .Upper and lower control arms, Coil springs/independent with lower control Arms, transverse-mounted leaf spring
Steering type . . . . .Recirculating ball, manual
Ratio 20.2:1
Turning circle, ft 39.9
Brakes, f/r . . . . .Vented disc/vented disc
Wheels, in. f/r . . . . .15x7.0, steel disc
Tires, f/r .F70x15, bias ply

PERFORMANCE
Acceleration, sec.
  0–30 mph 2.7
  0–45 mph 4.0
  0–60 mph 6.3
  0–75 mph 8.3
Standing quarter-mile, sec/mph . . .14.1/103.0
Braking, 60-0 mph, ft. 119

PRICE
Base price $4,320
Price as tested $5,542
Estimated current value . . . .$33,000–$35,000

'99 CORVETTE HARDTOP

GENERAL/POWERTRAIN
Drivetrain layout . . . . .Front engine, rear drive
Airbag . . . . .Dual
Engine type . . . . .90-degree V-8, liquid cooled, cast aluminum block and heads
Bore x stroke, in./mm 3.90x3.62/99.0x92.0
Displacement, ci/cc 346/56.7
Compression ratio 10.1:1
Valve gear .OHV, 2 valves/cyl.
Fuel/induction system . . . . .Sequential multipoint EFI
Horsepower, hp @ rpm, SAE net . . . . . .345 @ 5,600
Torque, lb-ft @ rpm, SAE net . . . . .350 @ 4,400
Horsepower/liter 60.8
Redline, rpm 6,000
Transmission type . . . . .6-speed manual
Axle ratio 3.42:1
Final-drive ratio 1.71:1
Recommended fuel . . . . .Premium unleaded

DIMENSIONS
Wheelbase, in./mm 104.5/2655
Track, f/r, in./mm 62.0/62.1/1,575/1,575
Length, in./mm 179.7/456
Width, in./mm 73.6/1870
Height, in./mm 47.9/1,217
Base curb weight, lb 3,153/1,430
Fuel capacity, gal 19.1
Weight/power ratio, lb/hp 9.1

CHASSIS
Suspension, f/r . . . . .Upper and lower control arms, transverse-mounted leaf spring, anti-roll bar upper and lower control arms, transverse-transverse-mounted leaf spring, anti-roll bar
Steering type . . . . .Rack and pinion, power assist
Ratio 16.1:1
Turns, lock-to-lock 2.3
Turning circle, ft 40.0
Brakes, f/r . . . . .Vented disc/vented disc, ABS
Wheels, in. f/r . . . . .17x8.5/18x9.5 cast aluminum
Tires, f/r .P245/45ZR-17/P275/40ZR-18

PERFORMANCE
Acceleration, sec.
  0–30 mph 2.0
  0–40 mph 2.8
  0–50 mph 3.7
  0–60 mph 4.8
  0–70 mph 6.1
  0–80 mph 7.8
Standing quarter-mile, sec/mph . . .1 3.3/108.6
Braking, 60-0 mph, ft. 116
Lateral acceleration, g 0.90
Speed through 600-ft. slalom, mph .68.1
EPA fuel economy, mpg, city/hwy. . .18/28 (est.)

PRICE
Base price . . . .$39,900 (est)
Price as tested . . . .$39,900 (est)

HOT NEW ROADSTERS: CHEVROLET CORVETTE CONVERTIBLE

CHRIS WALTON
Motor Trend, February 2000

This banana splits

I S THERE AN ICON more American than a Corvette convertible? Okay, we have baseball—the actual game, not the video simulation. We can't forget Elvis—Presley, uh, not Costello. Unknown to many, the "Corvette" moniker was first used by the British navy who so named its speedy, well-armed convoy escort ship in the late eighteenth and early nineteenth centuries. For its part, however, the Chevrolet Corvette has been part of American collective culture since 1953 and during its 47-year production has fortunately resisted fundamental changes that might have diluted the formula that now makes it what it is—unlike some other American neo-classic automobiles (e.g., Chevy Impala, Chrysler 300, and Mercury Cougar). The two-seater Corvette is and has been defined by a high-output V-8 (since '55, anyway) placed ahead of the driver in fiberglass-composite body where rear wheels drive. God Bless America.

Time and again, we've tested this all-American, fifth-generation Corvette (or C5), and each time, no matter how expensive or from where its competition originates, we've come to the same conclusion: The C5 delivers world-class performance derived from an enviable power plant (husky sound effects included), a communicative and balanced chassis supporting a highly tuned suspension system, a driver-oriented cockpit, and enduring supercar looks. And we're happy to report all this remains intact for the dawn of the millennium.

As far as manual convertible tops go, there simply isn't a better one around. Lined and including a heated glass window, the top doesn't look awkward when up, doesn't show at all when stowed, and doesn't require a bulky stretch-to-fit cover. Nor does it consume much room, still accommodating 11.2 cubic feet of cargo when down. To lower the canvas top, rotate two headliner levers, sandwich the front and back of the roof, pop the gorgeous hard tonneau, drop the top in, slam the lid, and that's it. All told, it takes under 10 seconds, with our best time of six seconds.

Despite lacking a wind blocker device, we found top-down motoring comfortably quiet and reasonably calm at normal highway speeds. The stereo's speed adjustable volume

Motor Trend editors gave the new electric banana color (millennium yellow) and five-spoke wheel design for the new 'Vette two thumbs up.

automatically recalibrates just right for topless travel, and the optional dual-zone HVAC system easily handles environmental demands. Its rock-solid chassis (this time around, it was designed from the start to be made into a convertible) is one of the best we've seen in any ragtop, showing hardly any deflection or telltale signs of cowl shake.

At the test track, we expected this car's standard automatic transmission to be a tick or two slower than its optional and more energy efficient six-speed manual. What we didn't realize, until we spied option code G92, was that this car was fitted at the factory with a 3.15:1 performance axle ratio instead of the 2.73:1 standard cog set. It's a $100 option that effectively makes up for lost time off the line by using a mathematical advantage—and it works. Our best 0–60-mile-per-hour time came in at a scant 4.9 seconds and a quarter-mile best of 13.4 seconds at 105.5 miles per hour is good enough to brag about—auto or manual shifter. Stopping from 60 miles per hour was equally impressive at a mere 113 feet (in the realm of the sprightly Porsche 911). You'd be hard pressed to find many cars that'd match that number.

Perhaps the most entertaining portion of our test regimen is the slalom course. As usual for Corvettes, our topless tester returned decent, though not earth-shaking, results: 66.5 miles per hour though the slalom and 0.93 g of stick on the skidpad. These numbers belie the fact that the C5 is one of the most neutral handling cars we've tested, and drivers who can find its limits are rewarded with predictable, throttle-on oversteer and precise steering to gather it back up again. By the way, with the new active handling system, the

Minus some of the goodies (head-up display, AHS, active damping, CD changer, etc.), the 2000 Chevrolet Corvette Convertible goes for $47,000.

While running the slalom course, the newest version of the C5 returned decent, though not earth-shaking, results: 66.5 miles per hour though the slalom and 0.93 g of stick on the skidpad.

GENERAL

Location of final assembly . . . . . . .Bowling Green, Ky.
Body style . . . . .2-door, 2 pass.
EPA size class . . . . .Two-seater
Drivetrain layout . . . . .Front engine, rear drive
Airbag . . . . .Dual front

POWERTRAIN

Engine type . . . . .90° V-8, cast aluminum block
 and heads
Bore x stroke, in./mm . . . . .3.90 x 3.62/99.0 x 92.0
Displacement, ci/cc 345.9/5665
Compression ratio 10.1:1
Valve gear . . . . .OHV, 2 valves/cyl.
Fuel/induction system . . . . .Seq. EFI
Horsepower, hp @ rpm, SAE net . . . .345 @ 5,600
Torque, ft-lb @ rpm, SAE net . . . . . .350 @ 4,400
Horsepower/liter 60.8
Redline, rpm 6,000
Transmission type . . . . .4-speed automatic
Axle ratio 3.15:1
Final-drive ratio 2.20:1
Recommended fuel . . . . .Premium unleaded

DIMENSIONS

Wheelbase, in./mm 104.5/2,655
Track, f/r, in./mm 62.0/62.1/1575/1,576
Length, in./mm 179.7/456
Width, in./mm 73.6/1,870
Height, in./mm 47.8/1,214
Base curb weight, lbs. 3,248
Weight distribution, f/r, % 51/49
Cargo capacity, cu ft, top up/down .13.9/11.2
Fuel capacity, gal 19.1
Weight/power ratio, lb/hp 9.4

CHASSIS

Suspension, f/r . . . . .Optional active handling system: Upper
 and lower control arms, transverse-
 mounted leaf spring, anti-roll bar/upper
 and lower control arms, transverse-
 mounted leaf spring, anti-roll bar
Steering type . . . . .Rack-and-pinion, power assist
Ratio 16.1:1
Turns, lock to lock 2.3
Turning circle, ft 40.0
Brakes, f/r . . . . .Vented disc/ vented disc, ABS
Wheel size, in., material . . . . .17x8.5/18x9.5, aluminum
Tire size .245/45ZR-17/275/40ZR-18
Maker/model . . . . .Goodyear Eagle F1 GS
 . . . . high-performance (EMT)

PERFORMANCE

Acceleration, sec.
 0–30 mph 2.0
 0–40 mph 2.8
 0–50 mph 3.7
 0–60 mph 4.9
 0–70 mph 6.3
 0–80 mph 7.7
 0–90 mph 9.6
 0–100 mph 12.1
Standing quarter-mile, secs./mph . . .13.4/105.5
Braking, 60-0 mph, ft. 113
Lateral acceleration, g 0.93
Speed through 600-ft. slalom, mph . .66.5
EPA fuel economy, city/hwy., mpg 17/25*
Estimated range, city/hwy., mpg 324/477*

PRICE

Base price $45,900
Price as tested $51,964

*Not yet updated to 2000 specifications
www.chevrolet.com

car initially attempted to compensate for our foolhardy slalom maneuvers by applying individual brakes to straighten out what the car believed to be a driver out of control. When we insisted we actually wanted to perform this at-the-limit exercise by not slowing down, the car responded by taking away our request for an ever-increasing amount of throttle. By the end of the run, we were casually traveling 59.0 miles per hour, despite having the go pedal buried in the carpet.

We love the new electric banana color (millennium yellow) and five-spoke wheel design for the new year—subtle they are not. Our tester was absolutely loaded with every option but polished wheels and came in just shy of $52,000. My neighbors about fell over at the price tag, but all this goodness minus some of the goodies (head-up display, AHS, active damping, CD changer, etc.) could easily be had for $47,000—that's a bit more like it. Just be sure to put a few dollars every week into your tire budget.

'VETTE VS. JET

Absurd? Sure.
That's why we did it.

JOHN KIEWICZ
Motor Trend, June 2002

JOHN LINGENFELTER is as good a Corvette tuner as any—actually, better than most. He's always happy to let us (and others) test his cars against all comers, bring what they may. So this time, we brought something that would give his latest road rocket a run for its proverbial pink slip. A hot Viper, Ferrari, or Porsche? Nah. How about an F/A-18 Hornet fighter jet? In this modern-day reprise of an '84 *Motor Trend* cover story, we celebrate two very different brands of performance: a ground runner that's fast enough to fly and a flyer that would surely own the land-speed record—if only it wouldn't leave the ground in the process.

Professional performance freaks live on one-upsmanship. A few years back, Lingenfelter Performance Engineering (LPE) built a 650-horsepower Corvette brawler that ran the quarter-mile in 10.8 seconds and didn't stop accelerating until our timing gear said 226 miles per hour (*MT*, March 2000). Shortly thereafter, Viper tuner John Hennessey upped the ante with a twin-turbo Viper GTS that cut a nine-second quarter-mile time, setting a new benchmark for the quickest nonracing car we'd ever tested (June '01). You can guess what happened then: a new twin-turbo smog-legal Corvette package from Lingenfelter. Car owner Steve Dumler's instructions to LPE were to not only up the bar, but raise it by a solid margin. Getting our Nomex fire suit into Dumler's 'Vette would be easy. Putting our arms around the jet would take a little more work.

"I've got a friend at the Pentagon," one staffer quipped. "Yeah, and I've got some contacts at the navy," added another. Soon we were calling/faxing/e-mailing whoever would listen to our ludicrous plan to pit the quickest (we hoped) street car we'd ever tested against a genuine fighter jet—the ultimate hot rod, courtesy of your tax dollars. After months of calls, we got a return call from the U.S. Navy's ultra-elite Blue Angels. This writer was volunteered for the mission.

"Let me get this straight: you want to race one of our F/A-18s against a Corvette?" asked a somewhat confounded Lieutenant Blankenship of the Blue Angels. "Well, yes," I

Motor Trend issued a challenge to expert Corvette tuner John Lingenfelter: Soup up a twin-turbo 'Vette to go head to head in a speed test against a F/A-18 Hornet fighter jet.

said, ever so casually. "And beyond that, we'll take the pilot for a ride in the 'Vette and then have him take us for a ride in a Blue Angels jet. Just for comparison sake."

Silence. Finally, the good lieutenant responded as expected: "Ummm, I'll have to get back to you on this." A few weeks passed before our phone rang again: "John, Lieutenant Blankenship here. On behalf of the United States Navy, you've been granted permission to perform your test. You've got one ticket to ride and one chance to acquire acceleration testing numbers on the F/A-18. Your pilot will be Captain Anderson. Can you be here on the 5th?"

PART ONE

Since we'd have only one crack at the Hornet, we thought it best to perform testing of the Lingenfelter twin-turbo Corvette beforehand. I packed my bags and headed for Dallas, Texas, the place Steve Dumler calls home. Steve's a hard-core enthusiast who has an impressive stable of toys, including tweaked Grand Nationals, Typhoons, an M5, a RennTech E55 and SL74, and what he refers to as his "Italian Chevy"—a Ferrari 550 Maranello. His newest wild child is this twin-turbo Corvette, which was delivered just a few days before my arrival. It looks remarkably stock on the outside and even more so under the hood.

Aside from a special fuel-pressure regulator, one would be hard pressed to tell that the engine was anything but original. However, hiding beneath those stock Corvette engine covers is a not-so-original V-8, good for more than 800 smog-legal (at least in Texas) horsepower on the LPE dyno. The original LS-1 engine was removed and stashed. A special 7.0-liter GM Performance Parts LS-1–style racing cylinder block was the starting point for an all-new 427-ci torque-monster. Special 4.125-inch-bore sleeves team with a custom 4.0-inch-stroke crankshaft, hence the 80-plus-cube increase over stock.

From there, an LPE GT2 hydraulic roller camshaft sends valve-opening cues to heavily massaged Z06 Corvette LS-6 cylinder heads. To top off the combo, a pair of Garret ball bearing–style turbochargers force in 14-psi boost in street trim and, given the right gas, can be programmed for 20 psi.

The engine package is remarkably smooth at idle, is quieter than a stock Z06 on the cruise, and passes the sniffer at the local (Texas) smog station. In street trim, generating solid acceleration numbers proved fruitless as the Lingen-vette would smoke its 345/30ZR-19 rear tires past 100 miles per hour. In search of traction, during testing we added a set of Mickey Thompson E.T. Street 26x11.5-16 "cheater slicks." Could this Corvette outdo the Hennessey Viper's stout 9.99-second record? It didn't take long to find out.

With 866 ft-lb of torque on tap, the key to a solid time is to, in drag-racer parl-

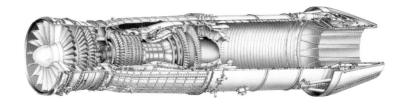

The F/A-18 made a high-speed run that a truckload of Lingenfelter engines couldn't: a Mach 1.25 strafing blast across the Arizona desert.

F404-GE-400

ance, "keep it hooked up," so I launched with a relatively timid 1,800 rpm. In spite of a bit of fishtailing and some nasty-sounding tire squall, the first run netted a 9.58-second elapsed time—breathing through catalytic converters, no less. A bit of fiddling and some adjustments to my driving technique brought even more impressive numbers: a best quarter-mile run of 9.24 seconds at 150.27 miles per hour. Perhaps more impressive, the 0–60-mile-per-hour run—the Holy Grail of acceleration measurements—took less than 2.0 seconds. No lie, no typo. Sorry, Hennessey.

So, how does a 1.97-second 0–60 run feel? Kind of like being hit from behind by a cement truck.

PART TWO

We arrived, ready for some more action, at the Naval Air Station in El Centro, California (near the U.S./Mexico border), under cloudless skies. It's easy to be impressed with just how professional our navy is. After a thorough vehicle search and I.D. check, we were escorted to the Blue Angels headquarters. The six pilots, who more closely resemble Olympic athletes than the movie hotshots dorkily depicted in *Top Gun*, were on the way out to engage in their morning flight practice.

The F/A-18 accelerated with a steady, strong, and smooth pull upon launch—a start that was more smooth than a Corvette's.

First up for me was a crash course (not my choice of terms) on the finer points of my role as ride-along ballast in a Boeing F/A-18 Hornet. The conversation basically consisted of, "Don't touch that, don't touch that, either, and *definitely* don't touch that." I was told what to expect during my hour-long ride and was politely reminded to grab for an on-board "party bag" if I felt an urge to visually re-examine my last meal. Truth be told, while my fellow *MT* staffers' sole objective was to generate good performance numbers via our Stalker radar gun, my lone objective was to not hurl.

Before long, I was suited up and strapped into the F/A-18. Captain Anderson versed me in the basics of the cockpit controls—at which point he informed me that I would not be flying it—and then asked if I was ready to pull some gs. Not knowing what I'd really gotten myself into, I naively bragged that "I'm the type

Members of the Blue Angels get to tryout the speed of a turbo-boosted 'Vette.

of guy who can ride roller coasters time after time without a problem." I felt quite confident I could handle the g-forces, inverted flying, and face-contorting directional changes encountered in typical combat-level flight.

Dumb, dumb move.

The twin GE F404-GE-400 turbofan engines fired up with a wail and soon began the cryptic radio chatter between pilot and ground crew. Salutes, taxiway directions, and signals were exchanged between the various Blue Angels crew members, their arms snapping rigidly, as if powered by heavy-duty garagedoor springs. We stopped at the "hold-short" end of the runway to allow time for our test gear to be set up for acceleration-data acquisition. After our test crew gave us the go-ahead, Captain Anderson applied full brakes, spooled up the engines, and hit the afterburners for what he called a performance-climb maneuver. The F/A-18 accelerated with a strong, steady pull, much smoother than I expected. The Corvette launches more violently than this. No biggie.

Before I finished thinking the word "biggie," the stoic, ever-professional Captain Anderson yanked the control stick and pitched us into a 5.0-g vertical climb as the engine's 32,000 pounds of thrust compressed my spine. This type of g-force saps the blood from a human's eyes, and that's no exaggeration; oddly enough, I could hear and feel but just couldn't see anything. As the F/A-18 leveled off, my vision restored, and I realized I was in way over my head.

The Lingenfelter 7.0L Twin Turbo V-8

My one solicitation of Captain Anderson was to break the sound barrier, so he radioed to the off-limits-to-the-public Yuma Range bombing area for some supersonic air space: "Blue Angel seven requesting time in the 2301." Luckily, my lifelong dream was approved, and soon we were ready to make a high-speed run that a semi truckload of Lingenfelter engines couldn't deliver—a Mach 1.25 strafing blast across the Arizona desert.

I must report that breaking the sound barrier was surprisingly anticlimactic. The F/A-18 rode steady, and there was absolutely no boom or shake as we punched right through the barrier. Captain Anderson reminded me that all the noise and sound-related turbulence were actually behind us; in fact, we were in front of all the action. Things got much more interesting when he said to "hold on" as he came out of afterburner at Mach 1.25. By now, I'd learned that when this guy says, "hold on," he really means, "hold on." The phenomenal amount of wind force and drag felt like a full ABS panic stop—when, in fact, it was simply a reduction of throttle.

Next up was a wing over, to demonstrate the zero-gravity environment astronauts feel. Special inverted fuel pumps were engaged, allowing up to 30 seconds of high-speed inverted flying. Before I knew it, I was upside down with my limbs flailing around as if I were a rag doll. Just as I was feeling a bit queasy, Captain Anderson quietly asked,

	'02 Lingenfelter Corvette	Boeing F/A-18 Hornet
POWERTRAIN/CHASSIS		
Drivetrain layout	Front engine, rear-wheel-drive	Rear twin-engine
Engine type	90° V-8, aluminum block/LS-6 heads, Garret twin turbochargers	General electric GE-F404-GE-400 low –bypass, turbofan-style engines
Valve gear	OHV, 2 valves/cylinder	7-stage axial flow compressor
Bore x stroke, in./mm	4.125x4.00/104.7x101.6	N/A
Displacement	427.6 ci (7.0L)	142 lbs./sec. airflow
Compression ratio	9.2:1	25:1
Hp @ rpm	802 @ 4,600	12,800 (est) @ 16,500
Torque @ rpm	866 @ 3,600	32,000 lbs. thrust @ 16,500
Redline, rpm	6,500	17,190
Transmission	Rossler 4L60-E automatic	A8 variable exhaust nozzle
Axle ratio	3.42:1	N/A
Final drive ratio	2.39:1	N/A
Suspension, front/rear	Aluminum upper & lower control arms, transversecompositeleaf springs, anti-roll bars	Oleo-strut
Brakes, front/rear	Brembo 4-piston calipers, 14-in. rotor	4-rotor carbon disc
Wheels, front/rear	LPE/HRE 18x10/19x12	10x6.6/14x11, forged aluminum
Tires	265/40ZR-18/345/30ZR-19 Michelin Pilot Sport	22x6.6-10/30x11.5-14.5 Michelin bias-ply
DIMENSIONS		
Wheelbase, in.	107.5	213.4
Track, front/rear, in.	57.4/60.0	122.4
Length, in.	176.8	672.0
Width, in.	70.1	484.8
Height, in.	54.0	183.6
Curb weight, lbs.	3,340	36,362 (no weapons)
Seating capacity	2	2
Cargo capacity	2 golf bags	Lots o' bombs
Fuel capacity, gal.	16.6	1,612

Boeing F/A-18 Hornet

TEST DATA	'02 Lingenfelter Corvette	Boeing F/A-18 Hornet
Acceleration, seconds		
0–30 mph	0.83	1.65
0–40 mph	1.20	2.26
0–50 mph	1.59	2.89
0–60 mph	1.97	3.57
0–70 mph	2.44	4.24
0–80 mph	3.06	4.93
0–90 mph	3.67	5.62
0–100 mph	4.33	6.32
0–150 mph	9.21	9.96
Quarter-mile, secs./mph	9.24/150.27	10.45/158.14
0–100–0 mph, secs.	8.75	N/A
Braking, 60–0 mph, ft.	108	Use the tailhook!
Skidpad, g	1.01	8.00-plus
Top speed	240 mph (est)	Mach 1.8-plus
CONSUMER INFO		
On sale in U.S.	Currently	You can't buy it, pal
Base price	$46,400	$28 million
Price as tested	$165,000 (est)	Don't ask
Air bags	Dual front	Dual ejection seats
Basic warranty	3 yr./36,000 miles	You're kidding, right?
Powertrain warranty	2 yr./24,000 miles	That's funny
EPA mpg, city/hwy	15/24	1.61
Range, miles, city/hwy	249/398	1,000/1,200
Recommended fuel	Unleaded premium	JP-5 jet fuel
	www.lingenfelter.com	www.blueangels.navy.mil

'02 Lingenfelter Corvette

THE BLUE ANGELS: A HISTORY

On April 24, 1946, the Blue Angels were established by Admiral Chester Nimitz as a flight-demonstration team to showcase naval aviation skills. Their mission remains to serve as positive role models and to enhance navy and marine corps recruiting. The Blue Angels perform at some 70 air shows per year and treat more than 17 million fans to fast-paced maneuvers and acts of flying precision (the F/A-18 jets fly just 18 inches apart, photo), including the renowned six-jet Delta Formation. Blue Angels pilots (and support crew) voluntarily apply for team consideration and, if chosen, spend two years training/performing and receive no extra pay. Many Blue Angels pilots have successfully completed Top Gun training and are generally regarded as the best of the best.

—John Kiewicz

"Enough light-duty stuff. You ready to pull some high gs?" My foolish retort? "You bet, show me what you've got."

Once again, really dumb move.

Part of my preflight indoctrination included learning the hook maneuver (constricting certain muscles to prevent the blood from leaving your brain and pooling in the body's lower extremities), which causes a happy-sounding blackout condition called "G-LOC." The next thing I heard over the intercom was "Get ready to assume the hook . . . ready . . . and go."

I'm proud to say that I saw 6.4 g, then took a quick g-nap. After 15 seconds of unconsciousness, I awoke to, "Hey, John, you with me? C'mon back, Johnny . . . hey, John, you with me?" I regained consciousness to be informed that we'd hit 7.3 g.

Back on the ground, the canopy opened, delivering a much-welcome blast of fresh air to my now Casper-the-Ghost-white face. Everybody laughed as I wobbled down the descent ladder. Let 'em laugh. I'd accomplished my two objectives: breaking the sound barrier and not launching my guts. A completely unfazed Captain Anderson strutted about as if the flight were merely a Sunday-afternoon drive. In fact, for him, it was. Even in my shaky state, it was easy to conclude that our fighter pilots are true athletes in every sense of the word.

A look at the test numbers reveals that the Lingenfelter Corvette conquered the quarter-mile in less time than the jet. But that distance is just where the F/A-18 really begins to gain momentum. It thrives on high-speed blasts, as evidenced by a stall speed (about 125 miles per hour)-to-Mach 1.0 (750-plus miles per hour) test that took us a scant 41 seconds. While the 'Vette generates an impressive 1.01 g on the skidpad, the F/A-18 can routinely deliver 8-g corners for as long as a human brain can retain blood. Clearly my brain was somewhat anaerobic on that day, but I did appreciate the once-in-a-lifetime opportunity to experience the seriously brutal power of a jet fighter.

Just for the record, none of the Blue Angels blacked out or needed a party bag during any of the numerous quarter-mile runs I dished up in the twin-turbo 'Vette, record-setter for us though it was. Wonder what we can bring next time? **MT**

AMERICAN V-8 POWER: 2004 CHEVROLET CORVETTE COMMEMORATIVE EDITION

JOHN KIEWICZ
Motor Trend, September 2003

The C5 departs with style

THE CORVETTE HAS ENJOYED a legendary presence and colorful history since its debut in 1953. The current, fifth-generation Corvette, now seven years in production, remains the most complete and potent Corvette package offered—though its reign will come to an end as a new, more aggressive sixth-generation car appears in '05. The C5 exits in grand fashion, however, in the form of an optional commemorative edition that celebrates Corvette's back-to-back class victories at the 24 Hours of Le Mans.

Available in coupe, convertible, and Z06 models, the commemorative edition emphasizes visual punch rather than power upgrades. Most notable is a special Le Mans Blue paint, the same hue used on the two C5-R contenders that returned to Le Mans this year and narrowly missed a three-peat class win at the famed endurance race. The commemorative package includes a special shale-colored interior; the seats incorporate Corvette cross-flags embroidered into the headrests. Also part of the mix are exterior badges acknowledging Corvette's Le Mans success.

There's one bit of CE hardware-related news: The '04 Z06 gets a race-inspired option in the form of a lightweight carbon-fiber hood that weighs just 20.5 pounds—10.6 less than the standard unit. This hood is constructed of unique, single-direction fibers intended to eliminate waviness, a trait common on painted carbon fiber. Atop the paint are silver stripes with red edges, similar to the stripe package used as a Le Mans—only aesthetic on the C5-R race cars (GM won't run these stripes at the rest of the American Le Mans race series events). GM says this is the first time carbon fiber has been used for a major body panel in a mass-production vehicle. "We definitely have technology transfer from [C5-R] racing to production with the example of putting carbon fiber into a series production street car that people can afford," notes Corvette Chief Engineer Dave Hill.

Apart from the commemorative package for '04, the Z06 receives specific chassis tuning upgrades intended to deliver increased performance and more vehicle control—all with a smoother ride around town. Considerable attention was paid to refinement of the

Sachs' shock valving in order to diminish the impact of yaw and roll, particularly in a series of tight corners. Ride/handling chassis engineer Michael Neal states, "We reshaped the force-velocity curve to give more control, but not at the expense of ride. What the customer feels, particularly on a racetrack, is a more poised car. He doesn't have to wait for body roll to settle during transient maneuvers, so he can be aggressive hustling from one corner to another, particularly as they come in quicker succession."

Added to the handling mix are stiffer upper control-arm bushings teamed with slightly softer rear anti-roll bar bushings to deliver flatter handling and more stability going into the corner, thus minimizing oversteer on corner exit. "If you want to fix oversteer at the back, you first need to fix it at the front of the corner," says Neal. Specifically, deterring oversteer requires generating a smoother entry, which, in the case of the '04 Z06, is noticeably easier compared with the '03 model.

The chassis refinements and reduced vehicle weight have paid off, as the '04 Z06 recently joined the ranks of the select few volume-production vehicles to have broken the eight-minute barrier for lap times at the 170-turn, 14-mile-long Nurburgring circuit in Germany, where Team Corvette performs development testing. This is a worthy accomplishment, considering that the exact same vehicle can then be driven cross-country in air-conditioned comfort, backed by a factory warranty.

Hill's goal for the '04 Z06 was "to make it the quickest Corvette ever produced," sending the C5 out with a bang. That it is and that he has. **MT**

Each cylinder on the LS-1 V-8 is fired by its own ignition coil located close to the spark plug, ensuring a crisp, strong spark for smoother idle, better overall combustion, and lower emissions.

At Michigan GingerMan Raceway road course, we had the opportunity to have C5-R driver Ron Fellows (multiple world champion in Trans-Am, World Sports Car, and American Le Mans) compare hot laps in C5-R and Collector Edition Z06 Corvettes. First up was the new Pratt & Miller C5-R, undergoing final tuning for the 2003 24 Hours of Le Mans. Familiar with the number 53 C5-R, Fellows blasted around the 1.88-mile road course in 1:15.07 seconds. With a Katech 7.0-liter V-8 pounding out more than 600 horsepower (plus a six-speed sequential box, Goodyear slicks, and huge brakes), the C5-R delivered phenomenal, repeatable performance—just what you'd expect from a multimillion-dollar championship team entry.

Next were some hot laps in an '04 Z06. Although it had been a few years since Fellows aggressively hustled a street car around a racetrack, his extensive experience in showroom-stock racing quickly emerged. With 405 horsepower delivered from the 5.7-liter LS-6 V-8, the Z06 has the torque to easily overpower the Goodyear street tires. So Fellows maintained a keen focus on cornering smoothness.

"I was surprised by the general balance," notes Fellows. On his third lap, he turned in an impressive 1:33.9-second time, proving the fortitude of the street-legal Z06 package.

"To really get an appreciation of what this thing's capable of, you need a racing seat. I found myself being tossed around quite a bit—the cornering capabilities are that good."

—John Kiewicz

	2004 Chevrolet Corvette Z06 C/E	2003 Chevrolet Corvette C5-R
POWERTRAIN/CHASSIS		
Drivetrain layout	Front engine, rear-wheel-drive	Front engine, rear-wheel-drive
Engine type	90° V-8, aluminum block and heads	90° V-8, aluminum block and heads
Valve gear	OHV, 2 valves/cylinder	OHV, 2 valves/cylinder
Bore x stroke, in./mm	3.90 x 3.62/99.0 x 92.0	4.12x33.98/104.6x101.1
Displacement, ci/cc	35.7/5,665	426.4/6,988
Compression ratio	10.5:1	12.2:1
Max hp @ rpm	405 @ 6,000	600-plus @ 5,800
Max torque @ rpm	400 @ 4,800	600-plus @ 4,600
Specific output, hp/liter	71.49	85.86 (est)
Power-to-weight, lbs./hp	7.70	4.23 (est)
Transmission	6-speed manual transaxle	6-speed sequential-manual transaxle
Axle ratio	3.42:1	2.70:1
Suspension; front, rear	Upper and lower control arms, transverse composite leaf springs, anti-roll bar; upper and lower control arms, transverse composite leaf springs, anti-roll bar	Upper and lower control arms, coil-over shocks, anti-roll bar; upper and lower control arms, shocks, coil-over anti-roll bar
Brakes; front, rear	12.6-in. vented disc; 11.8-in. vented disc, ABS vented carbon rotor discs	AP Racing monoblock 6-piston calipers, 15-in.; 14-in. 2-piece
Wheels; front, rear	17x9.5; 18x10.5 cast spun aluminum	18x12.5; 18x13.0 oz. forged magnesium
Tires, front, rear	265/40ZR-17; 295/35ZR-18 Goodyear Eagle F1 SC	25.5x12.0-18; 28.0x12.5-18 Goodyear Racing Eagle
DIMENSIONS		
Seating capacity	2	1
Wheelbase, in.	104.5	104.7
Track, front/rear, in.	62.4/62.6	74.7/76.1
Length, in.	179.7	182.8
Width, in.	73.6	78.7
Height, in.	47.7	45.8
Curb weight, lbs.	3,118	2,535
Weight dist., front/rear %	53/47	54/46
Cargo volume, cf	13.3	That's funny
Fuel capacity, gal.	18.5	26.4
CONSUMER INFO		
On sale in U.S.	Currently	Never
Base price	$50,000 (est)	Truckloads
Price as tested	$56,700 (est)	Bigger truckloads
Basic warranty	3 yr./36,000 miles	You are kidding, right?
Powertrain warranty	3 yr./36,000 miles	Call Katech, just for a laugh
Recommended fuel	Unleaded premium	100-octane unleaded

INDEX

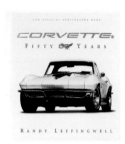
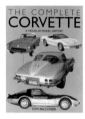
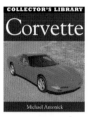

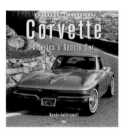

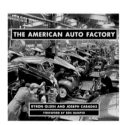